Monument of Gen. Edward Paine, Painesville, Ohio.

A Record of the
Revolutionary Soldiers
Buried in
Lake County, Ohio

WITH A PARTIAL LIST OF THOSE IN
GEAUGA COUNTY
AND A MEMBERSHIP ROLL OF NEW CONNECTICUT CHAPTER
DAUGHTERS OF THE AMERICAN REVOLUTION

Mary E. T. Wyman

HERITAGE BOOKS
2011

HERITAGE BOOKS

AN IMPRINT OF HERITAGE BOOKS, INC.

Books, CDs, and more—Worldwide

For our listing of thousands of titles see our website
at
www.HeritageBooks.com

A Facsimile Reprint
Published 2011 by
HERITAGE BOOKS, INC.
Publishing Division
100 Railroad Ave. #104
Westminster, Maryland 21157

— Publisher's Notice —

It is not uncommon to find errors in old books that were typeset by hand.
In this book, the page count jumps from page 63 to page 66.
No textual material appears to be missing.

In reprints such as this, it is often not possible to remove blemishes from
the original. We feel the contents of this book warrant its reissue despite
these blemishes and hope you will agree and read it with pleasure.

International Standard Book Numbers
Paperbound: 978-0-7884-1217-2
Clothbound: 978-0-7884-8813-9

PREFACE

N 1899 the New Connecticut Chapter, Daughters of the American Revolution, appointed a committee to locate the burial places of the Revolutionary Soldiers of Lake County, and to prepare a brief personal and military history of each.

At that time the number of known Revolutionary Soldiers buried in the County did not, perhaps, exceed ten or fifteen, and people best informed on the subject predicted that the most thorough search would not be able to more than double the number.

No sooner had the work commenced than the Committee began to realize the extent and difficulty of their undertaking. The length of time which had elapsed; the apathy of living descendants and relatives, when such could be found; the absence of grave-stones, and the loss of authentic records, were among the first obstacles to be met and overcome.

A thorough inspection of all burying-grounds, both private and public, was undertaken; local histories and town, county and church records were carefully studied; newspaper files running back three-quarters of a century were closely scanned, and in all cases the history of those whose age assured the possibility of their having been participants in our great war of independence, was untiringly sought out and brought to proof.

Much assistance was secured from secretaries-of-state of Mass. and Conn. and from the National D. A. R. The U. S. pension records, also, were indispensable.

All these sources of information, as well as others not enumerated, were constantly drained, while a persistent correspondence was directed toward officials of high and low degree, towards friends, relatives and neighbors, for proof of elusive facts and traditional statements. And now, after three years of searching and compiling we bring our labor to a close.

Should this little volume encourage other localities to undertake to wrest from oblivion and perpetuate the names and memories of those brave spirits who fought and suffered to found an independent nation, we shall feel that our long labor has been abundantly rewarded.

Mrs. Mary E. T. Wyman,
Chairman of Committee.

Painesville, Ohio, December, 1902.

JOHN ABEL, 1756-1836.

"Died in Perry, Lake Co., Ohio on Friday the 23rd of Dec. 1836, Mr. John Abel, a Revolutionary Soldier, in the 80th year of his age.

He rose in the morning in good health, ate a hearty breakfast, and went out and cut a stick of wood at the door; went in and sat down, and while caressing a little grandchild who was playing around him, swooned away and died instantly."

He enlisted in the Revolutionary War from Sharon, Conn., in June, 1777, for three months, under Capt. Jonathan Penoyer; Oct. 1st for one month, with Capt. Ephraim Meriner; Dec. 1778, three months with Capt. Amos Chapel; and again in July 1779, for three months, under Col. Lawrence.

His rank was that of Corporal, and as such he received a pension under the act of 1832.

He lies in Perry Cemetery.

STEPHEN AMES, 1748-1825.

Stephen Ames was one of the early settlers of Kirtland township, coming in 1815 from Hollis, New Hampshire.

He was at one time one of the selectmen of Hollis. He enlisted in the Revolutionary War in 1778 for three years or the war, in Col. Cilley's regiment. In 1818 the first township election in Kirtland was held at the home of Stephen Ames (one mile south of Temple) on Jan. 5th. Mr. Ames was elected treasurer, which office he held several years.

His son Jeremiah was made constable. He died Nov. 2, 1825; his widow Jan. 4, 1832. They are buried in South Kirtland, though no stones mark the spot.

He received a pension.

SILAS ANTISEL, 1749-1817.

Silas Antisel (Antisdel, A. Tisdel, Tisdel) son of Lawrence Antisel and Mary Armstrong, was born in Norwich, Conn. in 1749. He was married at Willington, Conn. to Maria Bethiah Curtis, May 4, 1775. From Willington he served in the Lexington Alarm, in the Revolutionary War, in Capt. Heath's company in April 1775, his brother Peres enlisting from Ludlow, Mass., in Capt. Isaac Colton's company, Col. David Brewer's regt., in 1775. The children of Silas and Bethiah Antisel were Curtis, Thomas, Peres, Lawrence, Silas, Thankful, Sarah, Hannah, Betsey and Bethiah.

They made the journey from Connecticut to Madison, Ohio, in the winter of 1812-13 with their son Curtis and his family, locating on the South Ridge in Madison.

Silas Antisdel died Sept. 13, 1817, and Bethiah, his wife, Sept. 18, 1824, and both are buried in the cemetery which was once a part of their farm.

One grandchild (Mrs. Don Wyman of Perry), born in 1814, is probably the oldest person born within the limits of Lake Co. now living.

SILAS BAILEY, 1754-1845.

Col. Silas Bailey, born in Mass. in 1754, died in Perry, Lake Co., Ohio, July 9, 1845, aged ninety-one years.

"Silas Bailey was a private in Capt. Artemas How's company, which marched on the alarm of April 19, 1775; service, twenty-four days. Also served under Capt. Jonathan Houghton during Oct. and Nov. 1776.

He was second lieutenant in Capt. Jonathan Marion's company, Col. Josiah Whitney's regiment."

Silas Bailey appears in the list of officers of the Mass. militia, commissioned June 17, 1779. He is buried in Perry cemetery, and is remembered here as the father of Rev. Jacob Bailey, a Baptist clergyman of pioneer days.

DANIEL BARTRAM, 1745-1817.

Daniel Bartram was born in Fairfield, Conn. Oct. 23, 1745. In 1777 he enlisted as a private in Capt. Hull's company, Col. Stearns' regiment, Conn. militia. He saw active service in the defense of Danbury against the raids of the British.

Daniel Bartram moved to Madison, Ohio, in May 1809, where he resided until his death, May 17, 1817. He was buried in the burying ground at Unionville, near the church. Soon after, the church was burned, and it was found impossible to locate his grave. A stone was erected to his memory in the Middle Ridge burying ground, where lie the remains of his wife and many of his descendants.

Contributed by Ida A. Mills, great-granddaughter of Daniel Bartram.

EZRA BEEBE, 1737-1813.

Ezra Beebe, it is said by some, was the first settler in Perry township, the honor being divided between him and Thomas L. Wright.

He died Jan. 15, 1813, aged seventy-six years. He enlisted in the 1st Regiment, New York line, under Col. Goose Van Schaik, in the Revolutionary War.

He was the first adult buried in Perry township, and now lies in the Town Cemetery.

WILLIAM BIDWELL, 1767-1831.

William Bidwell Sr., joined the 8th Conn. Regt. in 1782 under Capt. Joseph Jewett and Col.

Jedediah Huntington. His regiment protected the Boston camps and took part at Roxbury.

For nearly eighty years the Bidwell family was identified with the history of Lake Co. Wm. Bidwell with his wife and family of six children, came from their home in Farmington, Conn. in 1820 and settled on the Middle Ridge in Madison, which place was the Bidwell homestead for half a century.

Noah Porter, afterward President of Yale College, was their pastor and friend in Conn., and he exercised a great influence upon the trend of their lives, for two of the sons Walter and Oliver went back and graduated at Yale, studying for the ministry.

Walter H. Bidwell edited at different times "The Independent" and "The New York Evangelist." The Eclectic Magazine was founded by him. He was a traveller of note, and his book "Imperial Courts," was written after his presentation at the courts of Europe.

The other son, Wm. Bidwell Jr., remained on the farm, and was the main stay of the family, a good husband and father, honorable in all things. Of such stock was Connecticut's contribution to the foundations of good citizenship laid by the pioneers of the Western Reserve.

Two of the grandsons of the Wm. Bidwell, who served in the Revolutionary War, were in the War of the Rebellion serving throughout the entire war.

Dr. Theodore S. Bidwell was surgeon of the 125th Regt. of Ohio Infantry, and Walter H. Bidwell was a bugler in Battery C, 1st Ohio Light Artillery.

Wm. Bidwell Sr. died in 1831, and sleeps in the Middle Ridge Cemetery in Madison, near his home.

Contributed by Helen Bidwell Hoag.

BENJAMIN BISSELL, 1761-1841.

Benjamin Bissell enlisted in the Revolutionary War from Lebanon, Conn. in 1778 or 1779 in Capt. Bliss' Company, Col. Ledyard's Regiment for three months; again in 1781 for nine months in Capt. Munson's Company, Col. Zebulon Butler's Regiment, Connecticut Troops.

Benj. Bissell was born at Lebanon, Conn., March 31, 1761.

At the same place he married Elizabeth Heath in 1784, and later removed to New York, spending the larger part of their lives at Hartrick, where they raised a family of eleven children.

In 1832 Mr. and Mrs. Bissell were with a daughter at Burlington, N. Y., from which place he applied for a pension which was granted him. Later they came to Painesville, Ohio, to spend their remaining years with their son Judge Benjamin Bissell, where Benjamin Bissell Sr. died Oct. 1, 1841, and his wife Elizabeth, Feb. 24, 1851, aged eighty-nine years. Both are buried in Evergreen Cemetery.

Benjamin Bissell was a cousin of Gov. Clark Bissell of Conn., and his son Judge Benjamin Bissell was State Senator from Painesville in the years 1839-40.

BENJAMIN BLISH, 1753-1825.

Tolland Co., Conn., was the birthplace of Benjamin Blish, Feb. 22, 1753.

In 1774 he married Phebe Skinner, sister of Capt. Abraham Skinner of Painesville. He served as a private in the Revolutionary War, one month and nineteen days, in Capt. Micah Hamlen's Co., Col. Thomas Marshall's regt. from June 13, 1776, to Aug. 1, 1776; also twenty-five days, from Aug. 1 to Aug. 26 at Castle Island; also thirty-one days in Capt. Sylvanus Martin's Co.,

Col. Williams' regt., from Sept. 29 to Oct. 30, 1777, in Rhode Island; and again at an alarm at the same place for six days under Capt. Israel Hicks, Col. Thomas Carpenter's regt., from Aug. 1 to Aug. 6, 1780.

About 1780 he moved his family to Middlefield, Hampshire Co., Mass., where they resided till they left for Ohio in Feb. 1804, with his brother-in-law, Capt. Skinner. They traveled on the snow to Buffalo, and on the ice of the Lake the latter part of the way. He bought land and made some preparations for removing his family, returning in the fall to Massachusetts.

On the 20th day of June, 1805, he started with his family for Ohio. Leaving his oldest daughter, the wife of Orris Clapp, his family consisted of himself and wife, six daughters and two sons, aged 21 and 12 years. At first their journey was prosperous, but in passing through New York state, the father was taken sick with the ague, the roads grew very bad; after leaving Buffalo they found great difficulty in obtaining food for man or beast.

They traveled by short stages on the beach of the Lake, sometimes felling a basswood tree, and browsing the horses upon the leaves.

They reached Erie July 16, the horses badly worn and unfit for further use. Here they made an agreement with a man named Ross to bring the family and stuff to Fairport in his boat, in exchange for one wagon. The two boys pushed on with the horses and two dogs, enduring many hardships, before they reached the home of Capt. Skinner on Grand river, shortly before noon on July 20. They had had no weapon of defense larger than a pocket knife.

The family were on the way forty-one days, in jeopardy from winds and waves, sometimes a part of them carried ashore by one of the boatmen in his arms, then walking for miles through woods or on the sand, not knowing the fate of the others, till through the guidance of a kind Providence they all reached Painesville safely, July 30.

They went into one room of a log house with Esq. Merry until their own house was completed in Dec. 1805, on land yet known as the Blish farm, in Mentor. There lived for twenty years Benjamin Blish, rejoicing, even amidst the privations incident to a new settlement, that he had placed his children in a more desirable location than the Green mountains of Massachusetts, where his entire life had been one of severe labor and close economy, with no better outlook for them. He died March 11, 1825, aged 72 years. His wife died Oct. 5, 1844, at 91. They are both buried in the Blish Cemetery in West Painesville.

WILLIAM BRANCH, 1760-1849.

William Branch was born in Preston, Conn., Sept. 3, 1760. In the fall of 1776 when but sixteen years of age, he enlisted and was sent to old Fort Trumbull, where he remained until the following spring, when he was placed under the command of Capt. Leffingwell, to go to Rhode Island, but as his enlistment was opposed by his family on account of his youth, he was sent back to Norwich.

The lad, however, was determined, and on April 1, 1777, he enlisted in Gen. Washington's army under Capt. Jedediah Hyde, Col. John Durkee's regt.

He was engaged in the following battles, viz: Germantown, Oct. 4, 1777; Red Bank, Monmouth, June 28, 1778; Fort Mifflin, Nov. 17, 1777; and in other engagements and skirmishes.

During the winter of 1777-78 he was with Gen. Washington in the historic camp at Valley

Forge, and was in the forced march from the north to Yorktown, under the command of Gen. Hamilton.

He participated in the siege of Yorktown, being one of the soldiers selected from the Connecticut troops to make the final assault on the redoubt, and witnessed the surrender of Lord Cornwallis, Oct. 19, 1781.

He was present at the trial and execution of Major Andre, and was one of the three guards selected by Gen. Washington to take the body of Andre from the gallows.

On July 7, 1783, William Branch was discharged from Capt. Samuel Clift's company, in Col. Zebulon Butler's Conn. regt., at West Point, New York, and was honored with a badge of merit which he received from the hand of Gen. Washington "for six years faithful service," in the defense of his country.

His mind was filled with reminiscences of Revolutionary days, and he often lived over in memory and story the privations and sufferings of army life.

About 1790 he settled in Cayuga Co., New York, and while residing there was made Captain of a company of volunteers that he raised for the War of 1812.

He moved to Kirtland, Lake Co., Ohio, in 1834, and to Madison, Ohio, in 1837, where he resided until his death, Apr. 13, 1849.

His remains were interred in the Middle Ridge burying ground.

(Contributed by I. A. Branch Mills, granddaughter of William Branch.)

GARRIT BRASS, 1763-1837.

Garrit Brass enlisted for the Revolutionary War from Westfield, Mass. early in 1781, and served until Dec. 21, 1783, as a Private in Capt.

Banister's Company, Col. Newel's regt; also in Capt. Smith's Company under Col. Vose. in the Massachusetts Troops.

He married Lucy Matthews on Apr. 19, 1791.

He applied for a pension June 14, 1828 at which time he lived in Mentor, Lake Co., Ohio, where he died (or was burned in his log cabin) Nov. 25, 1837.

Old residents who remember the death think he was buried on school property long since vacated as a burial ground.

His widow received a pension also.

OLIVER BROWN, 1760-1845.

Oliver Brown, son of Zebulon Brown, was born at Stonington Point, Conn., in 1760.

May 26, 1777, at the age of seventeen he enlisted in the Revolutionary War for one year, under Capt. Eldridge; was discharged Jan. 12, 1778. Re-enlisting July 1, 1780, he was in service until Nov. 22, 1780.

He served with his regiment about New York, New Jersey, and Eastern Pennsylvania, and was in the battles of Brandywine and Germantown, and endured the hardships of Valley Forge. He was wounded in battle, and was guard over Major Andre for one "watch," on the night previous to the spy's execution, on Oct. 2, 1780. One night he halted Gen. Washington returning to camp without the proper countersign, and marched him to the guard-house, for which he was praised by the General.

In 1780 he married Mrs. Gracie Welch, and lived some time at Norwich, Conn.

His children were Oliver, Hosea, Dauphin, and Lewis, Hannah (Bliss), Nabby (Searls), and Patience (Holcomb).

The early summer of 1818 found Oliver Brown with his family located on military lands in Concord, Geauga Co., (now Lake) in Ohio, after a perilous journey with ox teams across swollen rivers, through an unbroken wilderness, ready to prepare a home in the far west. Mrs. Brown died in 1832; later he married Mrs. Beardsley who died in 1840. Again he married a Mrs. Hannah Perkins, who was left a widow by his death, June 5, 1845.

He was buried with military honors, and lies in the cemetery at Concord Center. He received a pension.

WILLIAM CAHOON, 1765-1828.

William Cahoon served his country in her struggle for freedom in the Massachusetts line, enlisting Oct. 11, 1781, under Capt. Samuel Sloan, in the regiment of Col. Asa Barnes, from Berkshire county.

He marched by order of Gen. Stark to Saratoga on an alarm.

He died in Kirtland, Oct. 1, 1828, aged sixty-three years, and is buried in Kirtland cemetery.

JOSEPH CALL.

Joseph Call, of Vermont, was in Capt. John Benjamin's company of militia, under the command of Col. Joseph Marsh, from Aug. 16 to Oct. 4, 1777.

He was also in a scouting party from Woodstock in the year 1777. He was called out on an alarm from March 9 to 12, with Capt. Jesse Safford's company of militia. His name was on the roll of men appointed by the committee of safety of the towns of Hartford, Lebanon and Woodstock, who watched and guarded suspected persons, as enemies to the United States of America.

He was also in Zebulon Lyon's company, employed in guarding the committee of safety to

Windsor, and Col. Stone and others to Springfield, service all in Windsor county, Vermont.

He removed from Vermont to Perry, Ohio, in 1815, and is buried in the South Ridge burying ground in West Madison. His son, Rufus Call, was in the war of 1812.

JOHN CAMPBELL, 1759 ——

John Campbell, a soldier in the Revolutionary war, served in the New York state troops.

He was a pensioner in Cuyahoga county until 1840, when Willoughby township was made a part of Lake county. At that time he lived with his son James, in Willoughby.

He was an early settler of Willoughby, being a prominent man there for many years, and has many descendants in Ohio.

It is a matter of doubt whether he died in Willoughby or while visiting in New York.

WILLIAM CARD, 1753-1820.

William Card (grandfather of Jonathan Card) died in 1820 and is buried in Willoughby Cemetery.

"William Card was commissioned master of 'The Schooner Phoenix' bound for Cape Francois."

"Boston, Mass. Nov. 21, 1776. By a petition to the council, signed by Mr. Card, in behalf of Daniel Pierce and Aaron Malady, owners of the Phoenix, said vessel was ordered for service in the Revolutionary War."

EZRA CARPENTER, 1764-1849.

Ezra Carpenter died Aug. 7, 1849, aged eighty-four years, eleven months, and twenty-eight days, and sleeps in Kirtland Cemetery.

His service in the Revolutionary War was at

an alarm in Rhode Island, Dec. 8, 1781, under Capt. Jacob Ide, commanded by Col. Daggett.

JABEZ CARTER, 1750-1836.

A soldier of the Revolution, Jabez Carter died in Kirtland, Lake County, Ohio, August 12, 1836, in his eighty-seventh year.

He lies in Kirtland cemetery where sleep several of his comrades.

He enlisted in Capt. John Walton's company, Col. David Green's regiment; was in the Lexington Alarm, and served his country until March 10, 1780, when he received his discharge.

CHRISTOPHER COLSON, 1765 ——

Christopher Colson was born at Weymouth, Mass., May 10, 1765. He enlisted in the Revolutionary War July 9, 1781, at the age of sixteen, and continued in service as fifer throughout the remainder of the war.

He served in Capt. Peter Claye's and Capt. J. K. Smith's companies under the command of Lieut. Col. Calvin Smith, 6th Mass. regt.

He was twice married, and with his second wife, came to Chagrin or Willoughby, Ohio, in 1810.

He was Willoughby's first postmaster, and walked to Washington, to secure his appointment.

He died in Willoughby, and is buried on the Daniels farm just east of Willoughby village.

TRACY CLEVELAND, 1749-1836.

Tracy Cleveland was born in Canterbury, Connecticut, in 1749, and died in Ohio, Feb. 27, 1836. Had he lived until May 8th he would have been eighty-eight years old. He is buried on the Harmon farm in Kirtland, Lake Co., Ohio.

In "Connecticut men in the Revolution" is the following service of Tracy Cleveland: "A private in Capt. Bacon's company, Sixth Battalion, Wadsworth's Brigade, Col. John Chester commanding the battalion in 1776.

"This Battalion was raised in June to reinforce Washington in New York; was stationed at Flat Bush Pass on Long Island, Aug. 26; and engaged in the battle of the following day; narrowly escaped capture in retreat from New York, and engaged at White Plains, Oct. 28.

"Was in New Jersey at the time of the battle of Trenton."

For his services he received a pension under the Act of 1832.

His wife, Phebe, died Nov. 5, 1829, in her seventy-seventh year, and lies by his side.

ROGER CRAINE, 1762-1841.

Roger Craine was born in Mansfield, Conn., May 4, 1762. He enlisted in the Revolutionary War from Medway, Mass., in May 1781, and served until Dec. 1783 as private under Capt. John Fuller and Col. Shepherd, and was in the battle at White Plains.

He married Sarah Whiton May 20, 1784 at Ashford, Conn. Their children were Abigail, Cyrus, Ahira, Eleazer, Tower, Horace, Alvin, Samuel, Alexis and Ruth.

They were living in Groton, N. Y. in May 1818, when he applied for a pension which he received.

Later they removed to Painesville, Ohio, where he died June 3, 1841 and in 1857 was removed to the cemetery in Mentor, Ohio.

This story is told by his descendants:

"Grandfather Craine had repeatedly refused to sign the temperance pledge, saying, he was not a drinking man, and didn't care to sign away his liberty. One training day an old drunkard cried out, 'Here comes Roger Craine, he is one of our set, for he will not sign his liberty away either!' Grandfather signed the pledge that day."

AMARIAH CRANDALL, 1759-1861.

Amariah Crandall was born at Westerly, R. I., Apr. 2, 1759.

He enlisted from Stonington, Ct., Apr. 1, 1779, for one year, under Capt. Sheffield, enlisting again in June 1780, for two months, under Capt. Elijah Palmer, and Lieut. Col. Richards.

During an engagement he was taken prisoner by the British, and sent on board the prison-ship Halifax, where he with the others had smallpox.

He resided after the war in Willington, Conn. from which place he applied for a pension Aug. 18, 1832, which was allowed.

He married Prudence Avery of Conn. Their children were Elijah, Elisha, Sarah and Daniel.

He with his wife came to Ohio in 1820 to live with their son Daniel, where they lived to a ripe old age, he being 101 years, 9 months, and 16 days.

His favorite pastime was telling his grandchildren Revolutionary War stories of Washington and LaFayette, whom he loved.

The family keep with great care his old bayonet.

He died Jan. 18, 1861, and lies in the Middle Ridge Cemetery in Madison, Lake Co., Ohio.

CHRISTOPHER CRARY, 1759-1848.

Christopher Crary was born in New London, Conn. in 1759.

He was the grand-son of Oliver Crary who was a native of Connecticut. His great-grandfather was Robert Crary, who was a son of Peter Crary who emigrated from England to America when Charles II ascended the throne.

Christopher Crary was a soldier in the Revolutionary War. He was twice taken prisoner; the first time he escaped from the Halifax prison, the second time, he was imprisoned on the British prison-ship Jersey, but was finally liberated.

He was in the marine service. After the war he became a merchant, then a farmer, and exchanged his farm for land in Kirtland township.

He was the first actual settler in Kirtland; his neighbors were seven miles distant.

In 1837 he moved to Union Co., Ohio, living there until his death, which occurred in 1848 at the age of eighty-eight years.

WM. R. EDDY, 1760-1841.

William R. Eddy was in the service of the United States in the Revolutionary War from Massachusetts, serving in Capt. John Wood's company, Col. Paul Dudley Sargent's regiment.

He was a resident of Concord, Lake Co., Ohio, where he died Dec. 14, 1841, aged eighty-one years, and is buried on the farm he owned, one and one-half miles northeast of Little Mountain.

He received a pension.

LEMUEL ELLIS, 1764-1859.

Lemuel Ellis came to Perry, Ohio about 1810. In 1815 he was overseer of the poor, and held that and other township offices until 1831.

From Dec. 11 to Dec. 30, 1776 he served in the Revolutionary War for Mass. under Capt. Ebenezer Battle and Colonel William McIntosh; later he was with Col. Weld at Castle Island.

He married Polly Call, and is buried in an old graveyard on the River road, in Perry township. The grave is marked by a boulder from Grand river which he had placed in the yard before his death which occurred on Sunday, Feb. 20, 1859. He was one of the earliest members of Perry Methodist Church.

JOHN EMERY, 1758-1831.

"Capt. John Emery died Dec. 27, 1831 aged seventy-three years."

He was born in Massachusetts, and from that state enlisted in the Revolutionary War.

He served many enlistments throughout the war, ranking as Captain at the close.

He was buried in the historic yard at Unionville, which contains the first authentic grave on the Western Reserve, that of Alexander Harper.

JOSHUA EMMS, 1751-1845.

Joshua Emms was a soldier of the Revolutionary War from Eastham, Mass.

He served in the Continental Line as Corporal, in Captain Solomon Higgin's company, enlisting July 13, 1775, discharged Sept. 1776.

"Joshua Emms was born in Boston, and was there when the tea was destroyed in Boston Harbor. When the British took possession of Boston, he was in service in the Fort, and the British destroyed his shop, furniture, all of his property."

He was among the early settlers of Perry, his name appearing in the township records in 1827. He died Dec. 1, 1845 aged ninety-four years, and is buried in Perry Cemetery. He was a pensioner.

JOSEPH EMERSON, 1754-1850.

Joseph Emerson, of Haverhill, Mass. was

born in Feb. 1754, living to be ninety-five years, nine months and sixteen days old.

He began his life as a soldier in the Revolution, at the first call, enlisting Apr. 16, 1775, for eight months, under Capt. James Sawyer, and Col. Frye, of the Massachusetts troops.

During this first enlistment he was engaged in the battle of Bunker Hill, which in his declining years, was very vivid to him, and he loved to tell the story of the battle, and of the part Gen. William Prescott took in it, to every one who cared to listen.

His second enlistment was July 1777, for two months under Capt. Aaron Osgood and Col. Lyman. He was a pensioner.

Joseph Emerson married Lydia Foster, who died in Massachusetts. Later he married Mary Hilton, who is buried beside him in South Madison, near the Gore church.

He is described as a "large man, six feet tall, with hair white as snow, reaching to his shoulders, which he always wore braided as in the olden time." On his tombstone is this inscription:

Joseph Emerson,

Died January 23, 1850,

Aged 95 years, 9 months, 16 days.

"I have a house not made with hands,
    Eternal, and on high.
Here my spirit waiting stands,
    'Till God shall bid it rise."

ORA EVANS, 1760-1845.

Moses Evans removed from Litchfield, Conn. to North Adams, Mass. where his son, the subject of this sketch was born in April 1760.

23

"At the time of the 'Lexington Alarm' in Apr. 1775, they, father and son were among the first to respond to the call. Taking their old flint-lock muskets from the wall, and such equipment as they had, they hurried to the relief of Boston, and all through the seven years war, they served as 'minute-men,' their last engagement being at 'Haarlem Heights,' and so pleased was Ora Evans with the country, that after he married he settled there.

"Ora Evans' mother followed the army as a nurse, seeking in every way to relieve the suffering, and tradition has it, that at one time, when a man couldn't be spared from the ranks she carried dispatches, which Gen. Washington wished sent to a distant office.

"This remarkable woman lived to be one hundred and eight years old."

Ora Evans was a pioneer of Madison, Lake Co., Ohio, settling there in 1812, on the County Line road, where he lived until his death in Feb. 1845.

He lies in an "old long unused brier-grown, cattle-trodden grave-yard" on the Ashtabula side of the road.

He is remembered as tall, florid, silver haired, and still erect, in spite of his eighty-five years.

JOHN FERGUSON, 1757-1841.

Capt. John Ferguson was born at West Farms, Westchester Co., New York, on Christmas Day 1757.

His father came from Scotland during the French and Indian War, and liking the country so well, he sold his commission and settled in Hackensack, New Jersey.

On the Revolutionary War records, he first appears on a muster roll of Capt. Job Wright's Co., Col. Van Schaick's New York Battalion,

"In Barracks at Saratoga," Dec. 17, 1776. Later he appears in Col. Morris Graham's regt. of New York militia, on a payroll for March 1778, and again in Sept. 1778. Later he was Captain of militia.

He came to Willoughby, Ohio, in the spring of 1824.

He married for his second wife, Mary Campbell, daughter of Finley Campbell, and was the father of thirteen children (two by the first wife); and grandfather of seventy.

He died at the home of Leggett Ferguson, on Willoughby Ridge, Apr. 4, 1841, and was buried in Willoughby Ridge Cemetery.

LEMUEL FOBES, 1754-1835.

Lemuel Fobes of Massachusetts was a soldier in the Revolutionary War, serving with the "Minute-men who marched to the Lexington Alarm; and later was in the battle of Bennington, his company having been raised to reinforce the Continental Army to the Northward."

Lemuel Fobes came to Painesville, Ohio in 1803 and settled near what is now Elm street.

He married Anna Bills of Mass. He was treasurer of Painesville township in 1813.

He died in 1835, aged eighty-one, and lies in Evergreen Cemetery in Painesville.

He received a pension.

ANDREW FORD, 1752-1837.

Andrew Ford, of Massachusetts, was born in 1752.

A soldier of the Revolutionary War, marching in response to the alarm at Lexington, in which he served seven days, in Lieut. Joseph Warner's company.

He was in the battle of Bennington, and was

also in the expedition to Stillwater and Saratoga.

He was a pensioner under the Act of 1832.

He lived in Madison, where he died in 1837, and is buried in the Middle Ridge cemetery.

ISRAEL FOX, 1755 ——

Israel Fox was born in Glastonbury, Conn., in 1755, and served in the War of the Revolution, enlisting in 1776 for three months with Col. Talcott.

In 1777 he again enlisted for three months with Capt. Hale, under Colonel Woodbridge, and another three months in 1779; also in June 1780 he enlisted for six months with Capt. Phelps.

He witnessed the execution of Major Andre.

In 1832 he was a resident of Mentor, Lake Co., Ohio from which place he secured his pension.

Those interested remember that he died in Mentor, though the burial place is not known.

SEBA FRENCH, 1761-1836.

Seba French of Massachusetts was one of the very early settlers of Painesville, coming in 1816.

About 1779 he married Miss Mary Ide and lived for a time at Clarendon, Vt., coming from there to Ohio. They had five sons, Daniel I., Warren, Artemas, William and Ezra.

He was a soldier of the Revolutionary War serving as private in Capt. Joseph Franklin's company, Col. John Daggett's regiment, in an alarm at Tiverton, Rhode Island.

For his service he received a pension, which at his death in 1836 was transferred to his widow.

He died Dec. 28, 1836, aged seventy-five and lies in the old Washington St. cemetery in Painesville.

NATHAN FRENCH, 1760-1847.

Nathan French was born in Massachusetts,

Feb. 1760 and died in Leroy, Lake Co., Ohio, Aug. 30, 1847, aged eighty-seven years, six months and twenty-seven days.

He enlisted in the War of the Revolution July 20, 1777 and served until August 7, 1780. He is buried in south-east Leroy.

He was a pensioner.

JOSEPH FULLER, 1758-1846.

Joseph Fuller Sr., son of Nathaniel Fuller, was born in Munson, Hampshire Co., Mass., May 27, 1758.

He enlisted in the 4th Mass. regt. and served all through the seven years war, as private, corporal and sergeant, in Capt. Keep's Co., 4th Mass. regt., commanded by Col. William Shepard.

He enlisted April 21, 1777, was appointed corporal in Sept. 1779, and sergeant in 1780. He received his pension as sergeant, first dated Sept. 6, 1819 signed by J. C. Calhoun, and later an increase bearing date Aug. 13, 1828, signed by Richard Rush.

He married Rachel Miller, of Bedford, Westchester Co., New York on Nov. 2, 1783. They made their home in Shoreham, Addison Co., Vermont, coming from there to Ohio.

He died Sept. 26, 1846, aged eighty-eight years, and lies in the burying ground on the North Ridge in Madison near his home.

JOSEPH GREEN, 1767-1853.

Joseph Green, the son of Ebenezer Green, was born Feb. 26, 1767, in Sussex County, New Jersey.

He enlisted in the Revolutionary War from Muncy, Northumberland Co., Penn., in Aug. 1779, to serve under Capt. Samuel Brady, for three months at Fort Brady, situated in Muncy.

During this period he was with several scouting parties, for Tories and Indians were hostile in the vicinity.

In May 1782, he enlisted for the war, in a company of Rangers commanded by Capt. Thos. Robinson in Col. Samuel Hunter's regiment.

To the same company his brother Ebenezer Green Jr. belonged, who was killed by Indians April 16, 1782.

Joseph Green did garrison duty at Minegan Fort, for three months, with occasional scouting raids, then at Fort Borley for five months, and was discharged the following December.

In June 1788 he removed to Chesining, Tioga Co., New York, where his dwelling was destroyed by fire in 1789.

He came to Madison, O. May 30, 1817. He received a pension from 1837 until his death in 1853, having spent all his life as a pioneer in new settlements.

He was a large man, of excellent character, and proud of the fact that he gave some service to his country in its struggle for independence.

The statement was made, at the time of his death, that he was the youngest Revolutionary soldier.

ELIJAH HANKS, 1761-1839.

Dea. Elijah Hanks was born in Mansfield, Conn., Aug. 30, 1761.

He served in the "Connecticut Line" in the Revolutionary War for eight months, enlisting March 10, 1778 in Capt. Allen's Co., 3rd Conn. regt., of which Samuel Wylly was Colonel.

August 14, 1782, he was married to Mary Walker, of Ashford, Conn., who was born Aug. 14, 1763.

Their children were Joseph, Elijah, Benjamin and John (twins), Esther, Clorinda and Patty.

Sept. 9, 1811, they left Willington, Conn. for Madison, Ohio, arriving Oct. 3rd when they immediately went to work to put up a log house (into which they moved Nov. 8) on the same farm which has ever since been in the possession of the family.

Other families coming into the neighborhood found a shelter at Dea. Hanks' hospitable home until their houses were ready for occupancy.

He died Feb. 11, 1839 at the age of seventy-eight, and lies buried in the cemetery on the hill in sight of his home.

OLIVER HARMON, 1756-1843.

Dea. Oliver Harmon, born in 1756, came to Painesville from Rutland, Vt., in 1815, where he resided several years, and then removed to Kirtland.

He married Mary Plumb, and was the father of two sons and two daughters.

He was a Revolutionary patriot, one of the "Green Mountain Boys" of Vermont, serving in Capt. Williams' company of militia, in Col. Thomas Lee's regiment, commencing the 21st of October, 1781.

He is remembered as a kind and benevolent gentleman, who died Jan. 9, 1843, in his eighty-seventh year, and is buried on the farm on which he lived.

He was a pensioner.

COL. ALEXANDER HARPER, 1744-1798.

Alexander Harper was born in Middletown, Connecticut in 1744. In the year 1770 he took a patent of a large tract of land and moved to Harpersfield, Delaware County, in the state of New York.

In 1777 he received a captain's commission

in a regiment of rangers commanded by Col. John Harper, the regiment having been raised by the direction of Gov. Clinton. He was afterwards promoted to the rank of colonel, and served with distinction in the War of the Revolution.

On June 28, 1798 he removed with his family to what is now Harpersfield, Ashtabula County, Ohio, and settled there, dying on the tenth of September of the same year. This section of the country was then a wilderness, and Col. Harper gave the township of Harpersfield the name which it has since borne.

It is said that soon after landing he placed his staff in the ground and dedicated a portion of the land as a cemetery, and he himself was the first to be buried there; he being the first white person buried in the Western Reserve, whose grave can be identified. An appropriate monument bearing an inscription with the name and date of birth and death, and recounting the virtues of the pioneer and patriot still marks the spot. This cemetery is on the county line at Unionville village.

A biography of this distinguished citizen and some of his first descendants may be found in an interesting history of Harpersfield, written by Mrs. Malvina Sherwood, dedicated to the Hon. Elisha Whittlesey, and recorded in the records of the Ashtabula Historical and Philosophical Society by the celebrated penman, the late Platt R. Spencer.

SAMUEL HAYDEN, 1749-1838.

Samuel Hayden, a Revolutionary soldier from Connecticut, enlisted at Goshen, in 1775. He was a sergeant under Capt. Sedgewick and Col. Hinman for nine months' service. He was also with Capt. Daniel Benedict's company, Lieut.

Col. John Mead's regiment, marched Aug. 12, 1776, was at the battle of Ticonderoga.

He was a resident of Winstead, Litchfield Co., Conn., later of Concord, Lake Co., Ohio.

He died in 1838, nearly ninety years of age, and is buried at Concord Center.

He received a pension.

AMASA HILL, 1763-1847.

A soldier in the Revolutionary War was Amasa Hill, born at Stillwater, New York, in October 1763. He enlisted from Spencertown, N. Y. in March 1780, for nine months, in Capt. Walter Vrooman's company, Col. John Harper's regiment.

He was with his regiment in the battle of Cherry Valley.

He removed to Ohio in the winter of 1809-10, settling in Madison. The exact date of his death is not known, but his will was probated Oct. 13, 1847.

He was buried in the cemetery near "Turney's Corners" in Madison.

He received a pension.

SIMEON HODGES, 1768-1838.

Simeon Hodges was born in Massachusetts in 1768, and died in Mentor, Ohio, June 12, 1838.

During the Revolutionary War, when a mere youth, he went with his uncle Capt. Isaac Hodges, in Col. John Daggett's regiment, from Norton, Mass. to Tiverton, Rhode Island and return, on an alarm call, making in all eight days.

He made several trips to "New Connecticut" as a traveling merchant, purchasing a tract of land in Newbury, Geauga Co., upon which his son Samuel settled in 1819 or 1820, and about 1822 Simeon Hodges settled in Mentor, where he spent the remainder of his life.

He lies in Mentor Cemetery.

JOEL HOLCOMB, 1760-1847.

Joel Holcomb was born in Granby, HartfordCo., Conn., in 1760.

He was of English descent, and at the age of eighteen years enlisted for eight months in the Revolutionary War. He served in the regular Connecticut Line under Col. Samuel Wylly from Apr. 26 to Dec. 31, 1778.

He married Sarah Warner and moved into Massachusetts, remaining there a short time; then to Onondaga Co., N. Y. where their five children grew up, and the oldest daughter, Sally, married Elisha Patch. Seymour, Fanny, Nancy and Marcus completed the family.

In 1820 Joel Holcomb and Elisha Patch, with their families, made the journey to Ohio, driving an ox team, the wagon containing their goods, and the young girls Fanny and Nancy walking nearly all the way.

Securing a heavily timbered farm in Leroy, Lake Co., Ohio, they went to work to make a home. All the privations of the early settler were theirs. Seymour died young, Fanny married James Wright, Nancy married Abel Washburn, and with the failing health of the father, who died in 1847, young Marcus became the head of the family.

Feb. 27, 1833 he married Lovisa Brooks, daughter of David Brooks, of Madison, to whom were born three children who survive him; D. M. Holcomb of Madison, Mrs. D. L. Palmer of Painesville, and D. R. Holcomb of Perry.

Joel Holcomb and his wife Sarah are buried in the Paine Hollow Cemetery in Leroy.

ASAHEL HOLLISTER, 1763-1839.

Asahel Hollister served in the Revolutionary War from Conn. in Capt. Elijah Wright's company, Col. Roger Enos' regiment, stationed on the Hudson river, at West Point in 1778.

In the Painesville Republican of Feb. 28, 1839 is the following notice of his death:

"Died in Kirtland, Ohio Feb. 12, 1839, Mr. Asahel Hollister, aged 76 years, formerly from Glastonbury, Conn., a revolutionary pensioner. Mr. Hollister made an early profession of religion, and joined the M. E. Church with which he remained for nearly twenty years, but left them and joined the Latter Day Saints (Mormons) about six years since, and died in the full faith of that doctrine. He has left a large and respectable circle of relatives and friends to mourn the loss of one who was a pattern of piety and Christian benevolence."

A resident of Kirtland since 1834 thinks he was buried in Waite Hill Cemetery.

THOMAS HUNTOON, 1753-1831.

Thomas Huntoon enlisted in Capt. Tilton's company, June 12, 1775 under Col. Enoch Poor, later in Capt. John Calfe's company, in Col. T. Bartlett's regiment of New Hampshire troops.

He was a resident of Sunapee, New Hampshire, and removing to Ohio became an early settler of Concord, Ohio.

He died Jan. 2, 1831 aged seventy-eight, and is buried in the Huntoon Cemetery in Concord, Lake Co., Ohio.

BENAIAH JONES, 1755-1839.

Benaiah Jones Jr., of Hebron, Conn., was born Aug. 12, 1775. He served on Washington's body guard during the Revoutionary War.

Feb. 7, 1781, he married Jemima Skinner, of Hebron, who was born in 1758, and who also did heroic work during the Revolution.

In 1782 they removed to Massachusetts, coming to Ohio in Sept., 1808, making their home in Painesville.

Mrs. Jones died in 1820, Benaiah Jones lived until Aug. 19, 1839, aged eighty-four years. He spent his last days with a son in Jonesville, Mich.

A monument in the Mentor Avenue Cemetery bears the names of Jemima Skinner Jones, Benaiah Jones, Elkanah Jones. "Soldiers of the Revolution."

ELKANAH JONES, 1761-1849.

Elkanah Jones was born in Hebron, Conn. Apr. 28, 1761.

He enlisted in the War of the Revolution in the fall of 1776, for three months, under Capt. Elijah Wright, and Col. Roger Enos.

In July and August of 1777 he was with Capt. John Skinner, and Col. Robert Lattimore. Again, in 1779, he was with Lieut. Noah Day for two months.

Enlisted again in May 1781, for six months, with Lieut. Josiah Burnham, Col. Wm. Ledyard's regiment, all service from Connecticut.

After the war he lived successively at Hebron, Conn., Newburg, N. Y., Middleford, Mass., Hamilton and Norwich, N. J., and later in Painesville, Ohio, where he died in 1849. He never married, and spent his last years with the family of Jonathan Goldsmith. He received a pension from the government and lies in the cemetery west of Painesville known as the Blish or Nye Cemetery.

EBENEZER JOY, 1764-1837 (?)

Born in Killingly, Conn., in 1764. Ebenezer Joy enlisted in the Revolutionary War at the age of fourteen.

He served four enlistments, dating Dec. 1778, May 1779, July 1780, March 1781; length of service twenty-two months, under Captains Nichols, Houton, Abel Stevens, and Jonathan Benjamin; and Colonels McClellan, Bartlett, Nichols and Wait of Connecticut.

He was one of the early settlers of Perry township, owning a farm on the River road, near the west Methodist church.

His name appears among the town officers as early as 1819. Oldest inhabitants remember his death in Perry, but we have not been able to get the exact date or place of burial. He had no children and received a pension.

Ebenezer Joy and wife were among the charter members of the Church of Christ organized at Perry in August 1829 by Elder Sidney Rigdon.

ABEL KIMBALL, 1762-1841.

Abel Kimball was born in Boxford, Mass., Oct. 10, 1762.

With his father's family he, when a child, removed to Rindge, New Hampshire, from which place he enlisted in the War of the Revolution in Col. Mooney's regiment, also in Col. Enoch Hale's regiment, and served therein until Feb. 1780. He was also an ensign, and afterwards a Captain in the militia. He received a pension in 1832.

He married Mary Parker, in New Hampshire, and then resided a short time in Vermont, but soon returned to Rindge, where he lived until 1809, then he removed to Jeffrey, N. H., living there until 1811, when he with his brother Lemuel came to Ohio.

Upon the death of his wife he married Abigail Cunningham. He had no children.

He died March 4, 1841, and is buried in the village cemetery in Madison, Ohio.

PETER MARKELL, 1765-1837.

Peter Markell was born March 24, 1765. He enlisted from Palatine, Montgomery County, New York, in April 1781, at the age of sixteen, and was discharged in November 1782. He participated in the battle of Johnstown, N. Y. under Captain Cook and Colonel Clock. He died May 25, 1837, aged seventy-two years and was buried at Kirtland, Lake County, Ohio.

December 9, 1792, he married Elizabeth Koch. Their children were John, Benjamin, James, Margarette, Betsey (Mrs. Banter), Peter, Nicholas, Mary, Fanny and Nancy who married Ezra Morgan of Geneva, Ohio, where their descendants still reside. The children are all dead; the last one, James Markell of Mentor, Ohio, living until April 1900. There are, in Kirtland, two children who are the great, great, great grandchildren of this Revolutionary soldier.

Peter Markell was one of the pioneers of Kirtland, coming with his family in 1816, bringing with him some of the finest horses that had ever been in this part of the country. In his later years he became an invalid, caused by privations and exposure while in the army.

His granddaughter, Mrs. Henry Booth, remembers him as a fine looking man, very kind and gentle with the children. She has in her possession an old-fashioned arm-chair, that he brought to Ohio with him, which she keeps as a souvenir. She remembers stories he used to tell her, one of which follows:

"At one time when his people were staying in a fort to be safe from the Indians, he was plowing in a field not far away. He had been advised not to leave the Fort as Indians were thought to be near. After plowing for some time, he became aware that there were Indians about the field.

"He dared not stop but kept at his work, though every time he came near the entrance to the field, he would stop and adjust the harness. The third time when he stopped he hastily unhitched from the plow, sprang upon one of the horses, and escaped to the fort, closely pursued by the Indians."

A young boy named Henry, a brother of Peter Markell, at the time of a battle between the Americans and British, went to the top of a hill that he might see the battle, and was lost; no trace of him has ever been found. His mother mourned so bitterly for her child, whose fate was clothed in mystery, that she lost her reason. It is said she spoke no word for a year or more. Mrs. Peter Markell lived to receive a widow's pension.

ISAAC MARTIN, 1757-1832.

Isaac Martin, born in 1757, died Nov. 6, 1832, at the age of seventy-five, and was buried in the Middle Ridge Cemetery in Madison, Lake County, Ohio.

He enlisted early in the Revolutionary War in the Connecticut Troops. He served in the first regiment of Gen. Wooster, in the ninth company under Capt. James Arnold, on the first call for troops.

The regiment marched for the protection of New York, and later engaged in the affairs of Lake George and Lake Champlain.

He received a pension.

ISAAC MESSENGER, 1746-1839.

"Isaac Messenger, a soldier of the Revolution, died in Concord, Ohio, on the 8th day of May 1839 in the 94th year of his age."

He served in Capt. Amasa Hill's company,

37

Col. Roger Enos' regiment, arriving in camp July 4, 1778.

He was at West Point and assisted in the construction of the first fortifications there, under the command of Washington, who was personally present a portion of the time. He had six brothers in the Revolutionary War, three of whom were at the battle of Bunker Hill. One of them, Reuben, was wounded at that time, but all survived the war.

Isaac Messenger's wife, whose maiden name was Anna Ward, and whose father was a Welsh emigrant to Connecticut, had three brothers who died in the Revolutionary Army.

Although born in Connecticut, Isaac Messenger's ancestors were French, having settled in Canada early in the seventeenth century.

Mr. and Mrs. Messenger, with their grandson Joseph Tuttle, arrived in Concord, near Little Mountain March 4, 1817, their son Ashbel Messenger coming in 1815 Among their descendants are Eugene Adams and Walter S. Tuttle of Concord, Rev. Warren B. Hendrix, late of Mentor, and Warren and George Hoose of Waite Hill.

Wade Adams, who died at Fort Thomas, Ky., Sept. 8, 1898, a soldier of the Spanish War was a great-grandson of this Revolutionary soldier.

Isaac Messenger is buried at Concord Center, and his widow, who died in 1850 at the age of 101 years, lies beside him.

PHINEAS MIXER, 1756-1821.

Phineas Mixer Sr., from Norwich, Mass., arrived in Madison, Ohio Jan. 24, 1805. He settled on a six hundred acre farm, on the shores of Lake Erie, near Madison Dock.

In 1811 he removed to Unionville and kept tavern in a log house, where now stands the house built by Phineas Mixer, Jr., and owned by his great, grandchildren, Don J. Barnes and Eliza Dorcas Pope.

His wife was Abigail Fobes of Mass. and their family consisted of five children, two sons and three daughters.

It is said of him that, "he was a man of sterling qualities, and active in promoting local improvements." In the Revolutionary War he was in the service of Massachusetts, enlisting Sept. 20, 1777 in Capt. Benjamin Bonney's company; discharged Oct. 14, 1777.

He died Nov. 3, 1821, aged sixty-five years and nine months, and is buried in Unionville, Ohio.

JOHN MOORE, Third, 1752-1843.

John Moore was born in Maryland, in 1752. He was in the service of the United States about seven years as a Revolutionary soldier, and three years in the Indian War.

He enlisted June 1, 1777 from Schenectady, N. Y. in the 8th company, 3rd regiment, New York Line with Capt. Leonard Blucher and Col. Peter Gansevoort. Enlisted again June 1, 1782 in the 1st regiment under Col. Goose Van Schaick; was discharged at New Windsor, near West Point.

He married Leah Groome, and raised six children, his son Isaac serving in the War of 1812.

He came to Ohio in 1810, settling in Kirtland, his family coming in 1811. Mrs. Moore died soon after, and was buried on one of the highest points of Kirtland township.

John Moore had some very narrow escapes from the Indians, the tomahawk of one grazing his ear, clipping off the top, the scar of which he always carried. He is remembered as a large, handsome man, the color-bearer of his regiment, and a great story-teller.

He died March 9, 1843, and was buried in Chester, where he spent the last years of his life.

He was a pensioner.

THOMAS MORLEY, 1758-1844.

Thomas Morley of Glastonbury, Conn., died in Kirtland, Ohio, Sept. 1, 1844, aged eighty-six years, and lies in Kirtland Cemetery.

During the Revolutionary War he served his country from Connecticut, enlisting in Jan. 1776, under Capt. Wells and Col. Cook, serving until Jan. 1777.

Again in Aug. 1777 he entered the same regiment for two months, under Capt. Bidwell; again, in July 1779, for two months.

He was in the battle of Stillwater.

Mr. Morley was one of the early settlers of Kirtland township. Arriving July 6, 1815 he began the settlement of his farm.

At the house of Thomas Morley, in 1818, was organized the first religious society in Kirtland. In 1824 this society erected its first church building, which was made of logs and occupied the site of the present Presbyterian church. Mrs. Morley died in 1848.

EZEKIEL MORLEY, 1759-1852.

Ezekiel Morley was born in Glastonbury, Conn., in 1759. Enlisted Jan. 10, 1777 to serve three years in the Revolutionary War, in Capt. Joseph Williams' company, known as the 1st company, 3rd Mass. regt, Continental Line, commanded by Col. John Greaton; was discharged Jan. 10, 1780.

He removed to Ohio from Genesee Co., New

York, in 1832, was placed on the pension roll May 2, 1833, which after his death was transferred to his widow. He died in Chester, Geauga Co., Aug. 6, 1852, lacking nine days of being ninety-three years old.

He assisted in erecting the first log cabin that was built in Cleveland.

Ezekiel Morley was one of the original surveyors of the Western Reserve landing at Conneaut Creek, July 4, 1796. "After a perilous journey by land and water. They christened the place Fort Independence, and celebrated the day with such demonstrations of patriotism as they were able to invent. They gave the National Salute with their fowling pieces, drank their toasts with water from Lake Erie, and blessed the land which they had helped to deliver from British oppression." He is buried in Kirtland, Ohio.

BENJAMIN MORSE, 1755-1813.

"Maj. Benj. Morse, Esq., born Nov. 7, 1855, died Feb. 6, 1813, age 59.
To every good he sought his aid to lend,
His country's, virtue's and religion's friend,
The morn shall come, this precious dust shall
    rise,
And songs immortal fill the immortal skies."

Thus reads the stone which marks his burial place in the old cemetery at Unionville.

"Benjamin Morse served in the Revolutionary War in the third regiment, with Col. Israel Putnam, in Capt. Obadiah Johnson's fifth company, on the first call for troops; was at Bunker Hill, also with the Quebec expedition." Conn. in the Rev.

He married a sister of Col. Alexander Harper, and is supposed to be one of the party that came with him in 1798.

41

JONAS NICHOLS, 1758-1843.

Jonas Nichols, a resident of Vermont, enlisted in Colonel William Malcolm's regiment, in the New York Line, in the Revolutionary War.

He removed from Vermont to New York, and spent his last years with his son Deacon Phineas Nichols of Perry, Lake Co., O.

He lies in Perry Cemetery.

STEPHEN NORWOOD, 1762-1842.

Stephen Norwood, of Massachusetts, was born in 1762, and died in Perry, Lake Co., O., August 1, 1842, aged eighty years.

He is buried in Perry, in the cemetery on the South Ridge, near the little Church.

He served in the Revolutionary War for eight months, in Boston.

CAPT. EDWARD PAINE, 1746-1841.

Edward Paine was born at Bolton, Conn., in 1746. He entered the Revolutionary service as an ensign in a regiment of Connecticut militia.

In June 1776 he became first lieutenant in Captain Brig's company and was a member of that company at the time of its retreat from New York to White Plains.

In 1777 he was commissioned lieutenant of the Fifth company of the Alarm List in the 19th regiment of Conn. militia, and later in 1777 was made captain of the same company and served as such until the close of the war.

He was later made Brigadier General of the militia in New York state.

In 1799 Edward Paine came to Painesville, from Aurora, N. Y. and purchased a thousand acres of land. The following year he returned with his wife Rebecca White Paine and eight children.

In August 1800 he was chosen one of the committee to organize Trumbull county into eight townships, of which township 11, range 8, bears his name to the present time.

In October 1800 he was elected to the Territorial Legislature, receiving thirty-eight out of forty-two votes cast, and becoming the first representative from the Western Reserve.

In 1801 or 2 he was commissioned by Gov. St. Clair to lay out a state road from Painesville to Chillicothe.

He died at Painesville, Ohio, Aug. 28, 1841, and is now buried beneath the monument erected to his memory.

ELEAZER PAINE, 1764-1804.

Eleazer Paine was the son of Stephen Paine, 5th, and was born at East Windsor, Conn., in 1764. Although young at the time, he saw active service in the Revolutionary War, enlisting as a drummer boy in Captain Bett's company, 2nd Connecticut regiment, commanded by Colonel Zebulon Butler.

He enlisted July 5, 1780, for six months, and was discharged Dec. 9, 1780.

In 1800 he came to Painesville with his uncle Gen. Edward Paine, but returned to Connecticut in the fall. In 1803 he moved his family to Painesville, and with Abraham Skinner laid out the town of New Market, which was the county seat of Geauga Co. until 1812.

Mr. Paine opened a supply store at New Market, but lived only a year after.

He died Feb. 10, 1804, leaving a wife, Aurel Ellsworth Paine, and six children. He lies in the old cemetery in Painesville.

AMAZIAH PARKS, 1758-1838.

Amaziah Parks, born in Sterling, Windham

Co., Conn., in 1758, served five enlistments in the Connecticut troops during the Revolutionary War.

He enlisted Sept. 1, 1776, under Capt. Jonathan Dixon and Col. Douglas. Again in 1777 under the same officers. In March 1780 with Capt. Jonathan Thompson. In the fall of 1780 under Capt. Titus Bailey, and again in Sept. 1781 with Capt. Bennett and Col. Bailey. He was in the battle of White Plains.

In Feb. 1798 he married Sabra Barrett at Alford, Mass. and removed to Mendon, Monroe county, New York, where they resided until 1818, when they removed to Perry, O., living on a farm, where the River Road joins the South Ridge.

He died Nov. 4, 1838, and was buried in the cemetery at West Perry, but was later placed in Evergreen cemetery in Painesville. He received a pension.

BENJAMIN PITCHER, 1767-1849.

Benjamin Pitcher served in the third regiment, Duchess County Militia during the year 1782, in the Revolutionary War, in New York State.

This regiment was commanded by Col. John Field.

Mr. Pitcher died in Kirtland, and is buried in East Kirtland, in what is called Angel Cemetery.

A brother of Benjamin Pitcher served in the war of 1812 both as captain and colonel.

JOHN REYNOLDS, 1760-1840.

John Reynolds was born in Norwich, Connecticut, March 16, 1760, and died in Mentor, Lake Co., Ohio, March 3, 1840.

He enlisted in the War of the Revolution from Norwich, was in the Lexington Alarm, also in

Bigelow's company of artillery; March 7, 1777, was a musician in the fourth regiment, Connecticut Line.

He was also a sergeant in Capt. Horton's company. He received a pension with the pay of sergeant, under the Act of 1818.

He is buried in Mentor, at Little Mountain.

SAMUEL ROGERS, 1766-1850.

Col. Samuel Rogers was born in Wendall, N. H., Nov. 13, 1766 and died in Concord, Lake Co., Ohio, Sept. 9, 1850. He was in the Revolutionary War for New Hampshire in the company of Capt. Samuel Richards, regiment of Col. Stark, for which he received a pension. He was married twice, first to Sally Pike, afterward to Rhoda Harvey.

He was also in the War of 1812, in which he received a Lieutenant's commission, but was always known as Col. Rogers, probably receiving that title from the militia.

He held the office of Justice of the Peace in New Hampshire, coming to Ohio in 1831, and is buried in Concord cemetery, near Fay's mills.

ISAAC ROSA, 1767-1841.

Isaac Rosa served in the militia of New York under Col. Abraham Culyer, in the Revolutionary War.

He was born Aug. 27, 1767, and died Feb. 27, 1841, aged eighty-two. He is buried in Evergreen Cemetery in Painesville, Ohio. He married Agnes Storm, and was the father of Dr. Storm Rosa, one of Lake county's earliest physicians.

ANSON SESSIONS, 1770-1827.

This pioneer of the Western Reserve was born in Windham, Conn., April 16, 1770, and died in

Painesville, Ohio, in August 1827. His father was a deacon of the Presbyterian church and a school teacher. Anson Sessions, in 1770, left his native place and went to Cooperstown, N. Y. After the defeat of the army of St. Clair he volunteered for military service under Gen. Wayne, and was with him on the Maumee, Aug. 21, 1794, when the Indians suffered such an overwhelming defeat that they never after made serious head against the whites in the north-west. After the treaty of Greenville, Ohio, he was ordered with the army to the Cherokee country.

Mason, the notorious leader of the banditti that infested the Mississippi country, was killed by one of his own followers for the reward offered. His head was brought in while Sergeant Sessions was at Natchez. While at the south, Butler, his colonel, died, and by request of that officer, made just before his death, Sessions accompanied Mrs. Butler and the children back to Pittsburg, then Fort Duquesne.

Being a soldier and a frontiersman, he was solicited by Aaron Burr to join his expedition, but suspecting its true character, he refused. Sessions was honorably discharged from the army after three years' service in the Indian wars, which on account of the part taken in them by Great Britain, were stated by Gen. Harrison in his speech at Fort Meigs, to be a continuation of the War of the Revolution.

For his services in the army a warrant for 160 acres of land was issued to his widow in 1851. It was obtained chiefly on the testimony of a Mr. Stevens of Montville, who was also in the army and one of the very few, if not the last survivor. During all the years of his service, Mr. Sessions used to like to say, he had "not slept under a shingle."

After his discharge he returned to Cooperstown, N. Y., where he lived three years; then started on horse-back, with a few hundred dollars in coin, for Tennessee, to buy a farm.

He stayed over night at Buffalo, there being at that place then two log cabins only, and following the lake shore, arrived at Painesville in October 1800, the same year of the arrival of Gen. Paine and Judge John Walworth. He was hospitably entertained by Walworth, and was induced by him to buy 180 acres of land, for four dollars an acre, now known as the Fobes farm. He immediately built a log cabin on the first hill near the river, cleared up most of the bottom land and a portion of the upland, and set out extensive fruit orchards. Mr. William Fobes, who died in 1860, told of eating peaches from this farm in 1806.

On the 16th of Dec., 1804, Anson Sessions married Asenath A. Fobes, a daughter of Lemuel Fobes, from Norwich, Mass.

A contract with the Conn. Land Company was made Nov. 20, 1806, and signed by Abraham Tappan and Anson Sessions in pursuance of which all that portion of the Western Reserve lying west of the Cuyahoga River, comprising over 800,000 acres, was conveyed. Mr. Sessions was not a surveyor, but was then a man in the prime of life, of great bravery and perseverance in any business he undertook, making him a safe and trustworthy partner. This statement was made by Judge Tappan in the Cleveland Herald in 1831. He also says that "Mr. Anson Sessions was large and well proportioned, and in his younger days decidedly good looking. He was a man of peculiar strength, and was known and esteemed among the pioneers as very kind and benevolent."

Mrs. Sessions survived him, with four of their six children, named Norman, Aurel, Mariner, and

Horace. He was buried on his own farm, where his remains now rest.

His name is inscribed on a monument in Evergreen Cemetery.

PELEG SIMMONS, 1761-1854.

Peleg Simmons of Middletown, Hartford county, Conn., was born June 3, 1761, married May 22, 1788, and died Oct. 1, 1854, living to be ninety-three years of age.

He was buried on Willoughby Plains, Lake Co., Ohio.

During the Revolutionary War he served his country from Connecticut as soldier on a war vessel, which was used to protect the coast.

ABRAHAM SKINNER

CAPT. ABRAHAM SKINNER, 1755-1826.

Capt. Abraham Skinner, descended, as family tradition relates, from an old English family, was born in Glastonbury, Conn., in the year 1775.

About the time of the accession of Charles the Second to the British throne, the family emigrated to America, feeling, in consequence of their having espoused the cause of Cromwell, and held office under him, that a more congenial home might be found in this country.

In the possession of this branch of the family, at the beginning of the past century, was a sword, which had been used by an ancestor in his service as an officer under Cromwell. This same sword again did valiant service at the time of the Salem Witchcraft Craze, for the descendants of this branch of the Skinners boast, that it was one of their ancestors, who dared to lead a squad of determined men to rescue from the gallows a poor woman, condemned to death as a witch.

Capt. Abraham Skinner, son of Abram Skinner and Phoebe Strong, was one of a family of ten children. Two of his sisters married pioneers of the Western Reserve.

Phoebe was the wife of Benjamin Blish, who settled in Mentor, and Jemima married Benaiah Jones, from whom the Goldsmith family are descendants. From another sister is descended the well known authoress, Elizabeth Stuart Phelps.

Of the early life of Abraham Skinner, we know but little. In the War of the Revolution, his military record shows that he served from the town of East Windsor, among the men who marched from the Connecticut towns, for the relief of Boston in the Lexington Alarm of April 1775, in Capt. Amasa Loomis' Company. Again, enlisted April 24, 1778, in Capt. Harrison's company, served eight months, and was Commissary of Prisoners, in the Fourth Regiment, Connecticut Line, Col. John Durke, commanding.

In 1788 he was married to Mary Ayers, resided for a time in Mulberry, Conn., and then moved to East Windsor. In 1796, as the agent of an association, he made a trip to England and returning brought with him three blooded horses, by name "Creeper," "King William" and "All Fours." From these have come some of the finest horses of Virginia and New England.

In 1798, Capt. Skinner in company with Gen. Edward Paine, came to the Western Reserve and made large purchases of land in Painesville and elsewhere on the Reserve.

In Painesville in conjunction with Col. Eleazer Paine he bought the entire tract No. 4, embracing about 3,240 acres.

Capt. Skinner returned to Conn., remaining in East Hartford until 1803, when he again visited his Ohio lands in company with the family of Col. Paine. They brought with them horses and cattle, farming implements and young fruit trees. They contracted for the clearing of lands, and built log cabins to shelter the Paine family, and one to be ready for the Skinner family when they should come.

Col. Paine and Capt. Skinner at this time, together platted out a town, embracing the site of their improvements, and located on the west side of Grand river about two and a half miles from its mouth. Much on the order of a New England town, this plot included a park or public square, and at the river landing a log warehouse was erected. This town was called "New Market" from the old Indian name *"Nemaw Wetaw."*

Capt. Skinner again returned to Connecticut, and in March 1805 started with his family, consisting of his wife, two daughters, three sons, and two hired men, for their new home in the wilderness. Their journey took them over the accustomed route, through the state of New York and as far as Buffalo. Thence by sleighs they came over the ice of the frozen lake. On the last day, between Ashtabula and Madison a team driven by one of the hired men broke through the ice, soon the horse ridden by the younger daughter, Paulina, (afterward wife of Nathan Perry, and mother of Mrs. H. B. Payne of Cleveland) broke through and was extricated with some difficulty.

They spent that night at Madison, and by the next day, the ice which had borne them up so well was unsafe, and they journeyed on by land to their new home, reaching it that same day.

Capt. Skinner was active in the interest of the new place, and other settlers shortly came in, among them the families of Joseph Pepoon, Benj. Blish and Benaiah Jones.

He made strong efforts to have the county seat located at "New Market," and the first trial was held in Skinner's barn. Soon a two story court house, built of black walnut logs, was completed by Capt. Skinner, where for several years, law and justice were meted out. At that time the whole of Cuyahoga, Lake and Ashtabula counties were included in the limits of Geauga county.

The first frame house of the new town was now built for the family of Capt. Skinner. Here lawyers, judges, members of Congress, and the early governors, met with the free hospitality of these old pioneer days.

This house is still in repair and occupied by a great-grandson of its original owner.

In 1810 Geauga county was diminished by two-thirds of its former territory, and in 1812 the county seat was removed to Chardon.

That same year Capt. Skinner laid out the

village of Fairport, and was one of the most efficient men in getting appropriations for its harbor.

It is said of him, that being a man of large means, and his farm always well stocked, he was thus enabled to be a source of some help to the poorer settlers, that "polite to every body and generous to the needy and suffering everywhere, Capt. Skinner occupied a prominent place among the people of his day."

A notice of his death on Jan. 14, 1826 at the age of seventy-one may be found printed in an early copy of the Painesville Telegraph of Jan. 21, 1826.

He was buried with Masonic honors.

In Capt. Skinner's direct line, the name has not been perpetuated, only the descendants of his daughters, Mrs. Mary S. Hine, and Mrs. Paulina Perry being now alive. Of his children's children but one is now living, Mr. Augustus Hine, formerly of this place, now residing in Los Angeles, California.

SAMUEL SMEAD, 1748-1842.

Samuel Smead of Deerfield, Mass., was born Jan. 18, 1748, and died in Madison, Ohio, Oct. 26, 1842, aged nearly ninety-four years.

He is buried in the cemetery at Madison village.

He enlisted from Deerfield in Apr. 1775, to serve in the Revolutionary War, as private under Capt. Joseph Lock. Another enlistment in Dec. 1775 under Capt. Leonard and Col. Woodbridge.

Again in Aug. 1776, for three months with Capt. Samuel Taylor.

In August, 1777, he was sergeant under Capt. Sheldon.

He received a pension.

MARAUCHIE VAN ORDEN SPERRY, 1754-1845.

Marauchie Van Orden Sperry seems entitled to a record among the brave ones of the Revolution.

She was born in Holland in 1754, daughter of Pieter Van Orden, came to New York in childhood, was driven from the city by Lord Howe's forces, married Lieut. Elizah Sperry in April 1779, died in Kirtland, Ohio, May 13, 1845, and is buried in the "Angel" burial ground.

Her father and two brothers were killed in the service, her mother died from the poisoning of their well by the British, who also burned their home and confiscated their estate.

She was a protegé of General and Mrs. Washington; was present at the capture of Burgoyne, and "assisted the suffering Americans on that memorable day."

The aid rendered to this publication by one of her descendants is done in her memory.

Her husband, Elijah Sperry (b. Sept. 8, 1751, d. Sept. 4, 1818), was Corporal, Sergeant, and finally Lieutenant in Capt. Osborn's company of Artificers, Col. Baldwin's Conn. Regiment. He was in the battles of Brandywine, Germantown, Monmouth, etc., and helped to make the chain obstructions in the Hudson River at West Point; he was a pensioner.

Contributed by her grand-son Harley Barnes.

JOSHUA SWEET, 1764-1840.

According to the Massachusetts Records, "Joshua Sweet of Deerfield received a bounty for enlisting into the Continental army for a term of three years, in 1781, at which time he was seventeen years of age, and is credited with service in Capt. Smart's Co., Third regiment, in July 1781."

He enlisted March 23, 1781, and served until Dec. 22, 1783, a part of the time under Captains Lee and Thos. Hunt, with Lieut. Col. William Hull.

In an obituary notice of Joshua Sweet in "The Telegraph" of May 7, 1840 is this:

"Thus has fallen a sturdy oak of the Revolution, amidst the storms and tumults of war, he stood foremost in the ranks, and in the defense of *Liberty,* a principle which he could duly value and appreciate, knowing full well its primitive cost."

In the village cemetery in Madison his grave is marked as follows:

Memorial of Joshua Sweet, a Revolutionary soldier, who died 2nd May 1840, aged 76 years.

CALEB SWEET, —— 1828.

Caleb Sweet came from the state of New York to Ohio in an early day, and was a resident of North Perry. While in New York he served in the Fourth regiment, Albany County Militia, in the Revolutionary War.

In 1817 he was an officer in Perry township, was justice of the peace until his death, which came very suddenly on March 3, 1828. He was buried on his farm in Perry, now owned by James L. Parml y.

JOHN SMITH, 1752-1836 (?)

"In November 1800, John Smith came to Painesville with his family. They landed on the beach at the mouth of Grand river, about the middle of the month. With the winter of a new country already commenced, without a home or provisions, they would have suffered had it not been for those already accustomed to pioneer life. They remained at the house of Judge Walworth, until their log house was built on the hill leading to the Arch Bridge east of Seth Marshall."

John Smith served in the Mass. Continentals, receiving a pension in 1818, at the age of sixty-six. His name appears on the poll books of Painesville township, each year until 1836, when he would have been 84 years of age, and it is supposed he died, though his burial place is not known. In 1803 he purchased a farm of 150 acres on the lake shore, now owned by the Fairport Land Co. just west of Shorelands, said to be the place Gen. Paine built his first house in Ohio. He held town offices.

BARTHOLOMEW, VROOMAN, 1761-1839.

Bartholomew Vrooman, a soldier of the Revolutionary War, was born in Holland, in 1761.

He enlisted from Schoharie, N. Y., in Aug. 1776, for one year in Capt. Ephraim Vrooman's company, Col. Peter Vrooman's regiment. Again, in May 1778 he enlisted for nine months under Capt. Pair and Col. Morgan, both of New York.

In the spring of 1779 he joined the militia, and was employed as a guard to the inhabitants while they worked in the fields, and in August of that year was captured by a party of British and Indians under Capt. Brant, conveyed to Montreal, and kept about a year. Afterwards he served in the militia under Capt. Hagar, various short tours and alarms to the end of the war. He married Hannah Mattice Feb. 15, 1792, and lived in Concord, Lake Co., Ohio, where he died Dec. 8, 1839, aged seventy-eight years, and lies in the Huntoon Cemetery in Concord. He received a pension.

JACOB TYLER, 1762-1847.

Jacob Tyler was born in Branford, Conn., enlisted in the Revolutionary War from New Haven, Conn., in the spring of 1779 for three months, under Capt. Mix and Col. Sabin; again, in 1781, under Capt. Enoch Staples, for six months; and again in 1782, for six months, under same Captain; later was stationed on the coast as guard, serving as sergeant in Capt. Aaron Foot's company, in Col. Hooker's regiment of Connecticut militia.

He applied for a pension in 1834 while residing in Broome, Schoharie County, N. Y. He married Abi Wheeler, Sept. 11, 1789 at Catskill, N. Y. He removed to Ohio about 1839, settling near Little Mountain.

He died Feb. 19, 1847, and is buried in Mentor Cemetery.

ASA TURNEY, 1759-1833.

Asa Turney, of Madison, Ohio was a soldier in the Revolutionary War, under Gen. Arnold; was in the battle of Danbury, Conn., when that town was burned by the British. He enlisted when eighteen years old, and served throughout the war.

He was born in Fairfield, Conn., in 1759, and emigrated to Ohio in the winter of 1806, being fifty-three days on the journey, with an ox team, following a wild trail through the woods, as there were no roads or bridges.

He purchased one hundred acres of land on the south ridge in Madison, which still remains in the family. He married Polly Downs, who died in 1835.

Asa Turney died Sept. 5, 1833, and lies in the Middle Ridge Cemetery in Madison.

WILLIAM WAITE, 1765-1844.

William Waite of Waite Hill, Willoughby township, died Oct. 3, 1844, aged seventy-nine years, and lies in Waite Hill Cemetery.

During the Revolutionary War he served in the Connecticut Line, enlisting May 26, 1780, under Col. Wm. Douglas.

He married Spedy Ferry, who died May 17, 1838, aged sixty-eight years.

EBENEZER WILSON, 1745 ——

Ebenezer Wilson was born at Swansea, Massachusetts (then Rhode Island) May 16, 1745. Enlisted in the War of the Revolution Dec. 8, 1776, to serve in an alarm in Rhode Island, in Capt. Robert Crossman's company, Col. George Williams' regiment.

He was twice married, and came to Ohio in 1812, buying a large tract of land in Mentor, Lake County. It is said of his son Samuel, who was stationed at Troy, New York, during the War of 1812 that he was the "Uncle Sam" from whom the United States received that title, first as a joke, but "has been in popular parlance ever since."

He lies in Mentor Cemetery.

MARTIN WIRT, 1760-1815.

Born in Germany and emigrating to this country at the age of seven years, Martin Wirt came at a time when the custom prevailed of selling out the passengers for payment of the passage money. He landed in Philadelphia, and was sold for a term of nine years, but at the end of seven years the purchaser died and Wirt was released. This occurred about the time of the opening of the Revolutionary War, so he must have been close to fifteen when he enlisted as a teamster in the army.

The only battle he is said to have witnessed was that of Brandywine.

At the close of the war he located on the Schuylkill river at Reading. He married Catherine Homan. They moved over the Allegheny mountains to Horseshoe Bottom, Fallowfield, township, on the Monongahela river, twenty-two miles above Pittsburg. Here they lived twenty-eight years, four daughters and three sons being born to them.

About 1806, two of his sons, Jacob and Samuel, went out into the "Indian Country" to look for a home.

They located some land in Hiram, Portage County, Ohio, and lived there during parts of three years. In 1808 they went back to the old home for their father.

He came into Ohio with them and purchased a farm and mill on the Chagrin river, owned by David Abbott. He was a man of quiet, unobtrusive mien, upright in all his dealings.

He died in July 1815, and was buried on a spur of the hill north of the river, in an old burying ground in Willoughby, Ohio.

EZEKIEL WOODWORTH, 1759-1839.

Ezekiel Woodworth was a soldier in the Revolutionary War from Massachusetts, enlisting from Hampden County, serving as a private in Captain Charles Colton's company, Colonel John Greaton's regiment, Mass. Line, from 1777 to 1780 inclusive.

He received a pension under the Act of 1818, which was later transferred to his widow.

In the cemetery at Unionville a stone bears this inscription:

"In memory of Ezekiel Woodworth, a Revolutionary Soldier who died Feb. 27, 1839, aged 80 years."

JAMES WOODWORTH, 1766-1859.

James Woodworth was born in Coventry, Conn., July 8, 1766, and died in Painesville, Nov. 2, 1859, aged ninety-three years.

He lies in Evergreen Cemetery. In the "Public Records of Connecticut" during the Revolutionary War, page 138 is this concerning James Woodworth, as verified by descendants.

"This Assembly do establish James Woodworth to be ensign of the fourth company or train band in the 12th regiment in this state."
~~worth to be Ensign of the of the fourth company~~

He will be remembered as the father of Harvey Woodworth.

WILLIAM WYMAN, 1765-1842.

Wm. Wyman Jr., was born at Northfield, Mass., June 16, 1765, and died in Perry, Ohio, March 6, 1842.

He was a soldier of the Revolution, enlisting from Putney, Vermont, in Jan. 1781, serving ten months as a private in the company commanded by Josiah Fish, in Col. Samuel Fletcher's regiment. The regiment was stationed at Castleton, Vt., and was commanded by Gen. Enos. In November 1781 he volunteered as a private in a company commanded by Capt. William Hutchins, and served again at the Fort in Castleton for two months, during which time he participated in a skirmish with Tories and Indians in which engagement he was wounded.

On May 4, 1799 he was married to Malinda Eaton, a daughter of Nathan Eaton, who was also a Revolutionary Soldier.

William Wyman Sr., married Margaret Holmes, of Scotland, who was left in the forests of Vermont with her three sons, the oldest thirteen years of age, while her husband and two older sons, Henry and William served in the war.

William Wyman Jr., spent most of his life in Vermont, following his sons Guy and Don to Perry, Ohio, where he and his widow are buried, she living until Oct. 16, 1865.

Revolutionary Soldiers Buried in Geauga County, Ohio.

Until 1840, Lake and Geauga Counties were one, under the name of Geauga, most of these Revolutionary Soldiers who were pensioners received their pension under the Act of 1832, while Lake Co. was a part of Geauga.

The primary work of New Connecticut Chapter was locating Lake County's soldiers, but in so doing, we have located by townships the following list for Geauga Co., hoping some one will be patriotic enough to make it a *complete* list, giving the military record of each, with dates of birth and death, and the place of burial.

Alden, David, Mass................Middlefield
Alford, Benedict, d. 1838, a. 82...........Troy
Barnes, Moses, N. J................Thompson
Bradley, Thaddeus, Ct., 1756-1840.......Burton
Benton, Zadok, N. J., d. 1835..........Chardon
Bridgman, Elisha, Mass...........Huntsburg
Carlton, Darius ....Huntsburg
Carter, Jason...........................Troy
Carter, Jonas, Mass.................Parkman
Cheeseman, Isaac ....Hambden
Church, Philemon, Ct..............Huntsburg
Clark, Ephraim, Ct...................Burton
Clark, Isaac, Ct ....Claridon
Cleveland, Samuel, Mass............Chardon

Cook, Marimon, Ct., b. 1761.........Burton
Curtiss, Reuben ....Parkman
Damon, Abraham, Mass.............Hambden
Davenport, Squire ....Hambden
Donaldson, Samuel ....Middlefield
Durand, Andrew, Ct.................Burton
Egleston, Eliab, N. Y................Auburn
Elliot, John, Mass ....Hambden
Fellows, Parker, Mass................Chester
Ford, Nathan, Ct....................Claridon
Fowler, Caleb, Ct., 1755-1822..........Burton
Gilson, Daniel, Mass., 1761-1845.....Middlefield
Gordon, Nathan ....Newbury
Hayes, Seth, Mass....................Burton
Herrick, Libeus, Ct..................Burton
Hopkins, Capt. Ebenezer, Vt., 1761-1838..Troy
Hosmer, Zachariah...................Parkman
Hickox, Nathaniel, Ct..............Hambden
Hutchins, Moses, Mass............Middlefield
Johnson, Benjamin, Ct., 1761-1825.....Burton
Johnson, Jonathan ....Russell
Kentfield, Ebenezer, Mass............Hambden
Kidder, Reuben, Mass................Claridon
King, Benjamin, Ct.................Hambden
Loveland, Frederick, Mass...........Newbury
Mastick, Benjamin ....Claridon
Morgan, Daniel ....Hambden
Northrup, Stephen ....Munson
Parks, Nathan, Mass..................Burton
Pease, Isaac, Ct ....Hambden
Phelps, Ira, 1763-1848...................Troy
Phelps, Seth, N. Y., d. 1826..........Parkman
Pomeroy, Ichabod, Mass.............Hambden
Pomeroy, Daniel, Ct................Thompson
Pool, Jepthah, 1751-1838...............Troy
Potter, Borden, 1764-1846................Troy
Quiggle, Peter ....Hambden
Rider, Benjamin, Mass...............Chardon
Russell, Gideon, Ct....................Russell

A View on Indian Point

Indian Point, located three miles east of Painesville, Ohio, at the junction of Grand River and Paine's Creek, is a triangular bluff, about one hundred feet in height, having precipitous sides, except the base which is on high rolling land. There are three distinct sets of earthworks, which vary in height from from two to ten feet, running parallel, and extending directly across the point, thus barring all attack. The entire tract is densely wooded, and large, pines are growing from the tops of the earthworks. This was undoubtedly a favorite Indian camping place.

Smith, David, Ct., 1763-1852..........Auburn
Smith, Josiah ....Claridon
Starr, Samuel M., Ct ....Hambden
Stocking, Reuben ....Hambden
Thompson, Lieut. Isaac, 1751-1823, Penn.
.... Middlefield
Trask, Retire, Penn................Thompson
Wells, Timothy, Ct., d. 1820..........Claridon
Wilson, Israel ....Montville
Witter, Joseph, Mass ....Bainbridge
Wilcox, Elnathan ....Huntsburg

Traces of these Revolutionary Pensioners in
Geauga-Lake Co. have been found, but graves
not located.

James Blair, N. H.; Serg. Jonathan Gardner, N. J.; Reuben Lake, Conn.; Samuel Heminway, Mass.; Nathan Ganson, Mass., d. May 2,
1827; John Green, Mass.; Joseph Lane, N. Y.;
Jonathan Pratt, Mass.; Oliver Robison, Mass.;
Peter Thompson, N. H.

Stephen Dun well, Ct., b. 1762, d. 1840; buried
on farm in Solon, Cuyahoga Co., O.; grave ob-
literated, served three years from Apr. 5, 1777 to
Apr. 5, 1780.

Cyprian Parrish, N. Y., b. at Fredericksburg,
N. Y., April 4, 1766, enlisted Apr. 1779; served
15 months under different officers, traced to
Genesee Co., Mich.

Mary Carll, widow of John Carll, of Maine,
who served in Mass. troops nine months in 1781,
under Capt. Pike, Col. Calvin Smith; d. at
Waterborough, Maine, Sept. 20, 1833.

Lydia Chappell, widow of William Chappell
of Conn.

Arter Graham, b. 1757, d. Oct. 29, 1841; not
verified.

View on Grand River. Lake County, Ohio.

Gov. Samuel Huntington's House—Built in 1810—Photographed 1902

New Connecticut Chapter Daughters of the American Revolution

(1) To perpetuate the memory of the spirit of the men and women who achieved American Independence, by the acquisition and protection of historical spots, and the erection of monuments; by the encouragement of historical research in relation to the Revolution and the publication of its results; by the preservation of documents and relics, and of the records of the individual services of Revolutionary soldiers and patriots, and by the promotion of celebrations of all patriotic anniversaries.

(2) To carry out the injunction of Washington in his farewell address to the American people, "To promote, as an object of primary importance, institutions for the general diffusion of knowledge," thus developing an enlightened public opinion, and affording to young and old such advantages as shall develop in them the largest capacity for performing the duties of American citizens.

(3) To cherish, maintain, and extend the institutions of American freedom, to foster true patriotism and love of country, and to aid in securing for mankind all the blessings of liberty.

These are the objects of the society called The Daughters of the American Revolution. The Chapter at Painesville, Ohio, bearing the name "New Connecticut," has in its five years of existence endeavored to carry out these duties in many practical ways.

Springing into existence just at the time of the war with Spain for the freedom of Cuba, the work of the Chapter centered on rendering assistance to our soldiers, especially Company M, of the 5th Ohio Regiment, which was recruited in Painesville. Time and money were freely spent to make their life in the swamps of Florida more endurable. Much aid was given the Red Cross Society; money contributed to the Hospital Launch "Missouri," and no opportunity lost to help bear the misfortunes of war, and to relieve the suffering.

Prizes have been given for the best essays on Historical subjects, by High School pupils.

The practical aid from the Chapter made it possible to

erect a monument to Gen. Edward Paine, a Revolutionary officer; the founder of Painesville, and the one whose name it had borne for a century.

Through the influence of the Daughters of the American Revolution, Painesville's Centennial was celebrated, and a historical paper published to commemorate the day.

Our soldiers in the Philippines have been remembered with books and money for the Ohio alcove of the library at Manilla.

A book-case in the Painesville Public Library holds many valuable historical works, loaned to, or purchased by the society.

The Chapter contributes to the erection of Continental Hall, in Washington, D. C., which shall be a lasting memorial to all Revolutionary soldiers and sailors.

During the five years of its existence, the society has given more than $500 for patriotic and benevolent purposes.

Its last work, though not the least, has been the locating of the Revolutionary Soldiers' graves of Lake County, and bringing to memory the lives of those men who achieved American Independence first, and afterward bore the hardships incident to the settling of a new country. It was a fearless spirit, coupled with necessity, that led them to undertake the dangerous task of subduing the western wilderness.

The name of the Chapter, New Connecticut, is an inspiration, being the first name given to this part of the country by the surveying party of Moses Cleaveland. On this occasion, the fifty men, women, and children of the party having landed at "Coyneaught" creek on Monday, July 4, 1796, after a perilous journey by land and water, ranged themselves on the beach of old Lake Erie, and fired a Federal salute of fifteen rounds, and then in honor of the new state, to be founded, they fired a sixteenth to the name of "New Connecticut."

As we offer the results of our labors to an indulgent public, we feel that it is not inappropriate to allude to, and commend the earnest, the patriotic, the sisterly spirit that has at all times pervaded and characterized our chapter, and to look forward to a continuation of such valuable and appropriate work in our special lines, as such a spirit alone is able to insure.

Membership Roll of New Connecticut Chapter, Daughters of the American Revolution, Painesville Ohio, 1902.

ADAMS, GRACE ABIGAIL, Nat. No. 31,051, Painesville, O.

Great-great-granddaughter of Moses Adams, who enlisted for three years in a Mass. Regt. and whose name appears as Corporal and Sergeant. Died June 28, 1778.

ALVORD, MRS. HELEN HINE, Nat. No. 24,891, Painesville, O.

Great-granddaughter of Noble Hine, who was Capt. of a company during the Danbury Raid, Apr. 25-28, 1777; and who also turned out to repel the enemy at New Haven, July 5, 1779; Tryon's Invasion.

Great-granddaughter of Abraham Skinner, who was a Private in Captain Amasa Loomis' Co., and who marched to the relief of Boston in the Lexington Alarm, Apr. 19, 1775. Enlisted again Apr. 24, 1778 for eight months.

AVERY, MRS. IONE LESTER, Nat. No. 24,288, Cleveland, O.

Great-great-granddaughter of Samuel Lester Jr. Great-granddaughter of Benajah Lester. Father and son, both of whom enlisted as Privates in Capt. Gallup's company, in Eighth Regiment at New York, Sept 8, 1776. Discharged Nov. 9 and 17, 1776.

AVERY, EVELYN, Nat. No. 21,271, Cleveland, Ohio.

Great-great-granddaughter of Daniel Starr, who was born in 1724, and was in the expedition for the relief of Fort William Henry in 1757; was Major in the Continental Army, and lost his life by an accident, Apr. 27, 1777, at Danbury, Conn., just after his return from a relief expedition to New York City.

Great-granddaughter of Frederick Jones Whiting, (son-in-law of the above) born 1757, died 1804. He was a Lieut. in Conn. Troops; was a member of the order of Cincinnatus, his certificate of membership signed by Generals Knox and Washington being in existence.

Great-granddaughter of Nathan Avery, who was a Private in Capt. Samuel Holding Parson's 1st Co. at New London, Conn.; was at Bunker Hill; in 1776 a Private in Capt. Edward Mott's Co. for defence of New London Harbor; a pensioner.

BAKER, MRS. MARY AUGUSTA WOLFF, Nat. No. 33,533, Painesville, O.

Great-great-granddaughter of Christopher Truby, who was a civil officer, and Capt. of Westmoreland Co., Penn. Militia, served in the War of the Revolution.

Great-granddaughter of Samuel Murphy, who enlisted as Private in the 8th Virginia Regt; again for three years in 13th Virginia Regt; in 1781 was captured by Indians, sold to the British, who imprisoned him on an island in the St. Lawrence River, from which he escaped in 1782.

Great-granddaughter of Jacob Wolff, a pensioner of Armstrong Co., Penn; he also received a grant of land; was at the battles of Germantown, Brandywine, and wintered at Valley Forge.

BARTHOLOMEW, MRS. FLORENCE, Nat.
No. 39,724, Huntsburg, O.

Great-granddaughter of Childs Taylor, a soldier in the War of the Revolution, stationed at Ticonderoga, also at Montreal, Canada; later was at Germantown and Princeton.

BARROWS, MRS. GERTRUDE WYMAN, Nat. No. 41,057, Painesville, O.

Great-granddaughter of William Wyman Sr., Granddaughter of William Wyman Jr., who were privates in Capt. Fish's Co., Col. Fletcher's Battalion in the service of Vermont, also in Capt. Whitney's company of Vermont Militia. Wm. Wyman Jr. was also a private in Capt. Hutchin's company, Vermont Troops stationed at Fort Castleton where he was wounded in a skirmish with Tories and Indians.

Great-granddaughter of Nathan Eaton, who was a private in Capt. Marcy's Co., Col. Chester's Connecticut Regiment; served in New Jersey in the battles of Trenton and Stony Point.

A pensioner.

Great-granddaughter of Silas Antisdel, who was a private in Capt. Ebenezer Heath's company, from the town of Willington, Conn. for the relief of Boston in the "Lexington Alarm," Apr. 1775.

Great-granddaughter of James Parker, who, in March 1781, joined the Battalion under Brig. Gen. Waterbury, which was raised to defend the sea coast from Horse Neck to New Haven inclusive, and in July joined Washington while he was encamped at Phillipsburg.

BLACKMON, MRS. LUCY MATHEWS, Nat.
No. 21,265, Painesville, O.

Great-great-granddaughter of Thomas Dean, who served as corporal at the battle of Bunker

Hill, and on other occasions as Sergeant, Lieutenant and Captain in Col. Girdley's Regiment of Artillery at Boston. He was born Aug. 6, 1754, and enlisted in May 1775. In Oct. 1778 he went to sea, and was taken prisoner by the British, and carried to the Barbadoes Islands, where he was killed by a hurricane in March 1780, aged 26 years.

Great-great-great-granddaughter of Jabez Huntington, born in Norwich, Conn., Aug. 2, 1719. A graduate of Yale, and in May 1750 was elected to the Connecticut House of Representatives in the General Assembly. He was speaker of the House until May 1764.

In the Revolutionary War he was one of the Council of Safety and Maj. Gen. of Militia until poor health compelled him to resign all offices. After seven years illness he died Oct. 5, 1786.

BURROWS, MRS. CLARA E. WOODRUFF,
Nat. No., 21,260, Painesville, O.

Granddaughter of Gedor Woodruff, who served three years and three months as private in Connecticut Regiments and participated in the battle of Fort Independence. Was a pensioner under the first general pension act of 1818.

CARPENTER, MRS. ANNIE MILLER, Nat.
No. 21,261, Painesville, O.

Great-great-granddaughter of George Herkimer, who was a member of the "Committee of Safety;" was Captain of 8th Company, 4th Battalion, Tryon County Militia and Colonel of Minute Men under command of General Herkimer.

COLLACOTT, MRS. MARY HOVER, Nat. No.
31,052, Painesville, O.

Great-great-granddaughter of Edward Paine,

who served as ensign in a company of Connecticut Militia. Was afterward First Lieutenant; then Captain, serving as such until the close of the War; was in active service more than two years; was a pensioner.

Great-great-granddaughter of Eleazer Paine, who enlisted July 5, 1780 in Capt. Bett's Co., 2nd Connecticut Regt., commanded by Col. Zebulon Butler for six months as a drummer; discharged Dec. 9, 1780. Born 1764, died 1804.

Great-great-great-granddaughter of Stephen Paine, who served as a private in Captain John Spurr's Company, 6th Massachusetts Regiment, commanded by Colonel Thomas Nixon, in the Revolutionary War.

He enlisted Feb. 1, 1777, for three years, and was discharged Feb. 1, 1780. He witnessed the surrender of Burgoyne.

CUMINGS, JULIA ALICE, Nat. No. 2,616.

CUMINGS, STELLA LOUISE, Nat. No. 37,847, Painesville, O.

Great-great-granddaughters of Joseph Kingsbury, who was a member of the Connecticut General Assembly from 1777 to 1785; was a delegate from Enfield, Conn. to the Convention to ratify the Constitution of the United States.

Great-granddaughters of Benj. Cumings Sr., a Lieut. in the New Hampshire Continental Regiments from Hollis, who served in the Lexington Campaign in 1775 and in the Cambridge campaign for 8 months in 1775 and in the Continental Army one year 1776.

Great-granddaughters of John Whitaker, a private in Walker's Company of New Hampshire Militia.

Great-granddaughters of Jacob Hill, who served as private in Massachusetts Regiment.

Great- granddaughters of William Poole, who participated in the capture of Ticonderoga.

Great-granddaughters of Lemuel Kingsbury, who assisted in the Lexington Alarm, and later became Lieut. in the 5th Regiment, Light Horse, 1776-1778.

DANIELSON, MRS. NELLIE V., Nat. No. 26,245, Erie, Penn. Transferred to Presque Isle Chapter.

Great-granddaughter of Christopher Colson, who enlisted July 9, 1781 as fifer, and served in Captain Peter Claye's and Captain J. K. Smith's companies, under the command of Lieut. Colonel Calvin Smith in the 6th Massachusetts Regiment.

Great-granddaughter of Ebenezer Wilson, who served in an alarm in Rhode Island in Capt. Robert Crosman's company, Col. George Williams' Regiment. Born at Swansea, Mass., May 16, 1745. Enlisted Dec. 8, 1776.

Great-great-granddaughter of Israel Fox, who enlisted in 1776 for three months with Col. Talcott; again in 1777 for three months with Capt. Hale, and Col. Woodbridge; three months in 1779; in June 1780 he enlisted for six months with Capt. Phelps. He witnessed the execution of Maj. Andre.

Born in Glastonbury, Conn. in 1755.

DARROW, MRS. ADELIA ˟ FIELD, Nat. No. 35,538, Painesville, O.

Great-great-granddaughter of David Field, whose name appears on a list of Field Officers of the Massachusetts Militia, as Colonel of the 5th Hampshire County Regiment. Commissioned Feb. 8, 1776.

FOWLER, MRS. MARY M. DONALDSON.
  Nat. No. 24,892, Painesville, O.

Great-granddaughter of Jonathan Fish, a private in Captain Moses Branch's company of Connecticut men in the Revolutionary War; entered the service Jan. 8, 1778.

FORD, MRS. CONNIE E., Nat. No. 41,560,
  Burton, O.

Great-granddaughter of Thaddeus Bradley, who was a private in the War of the Revolution, enlisting at Cheshire, Conn., in May 1775 under Capt. Josiah Wright, and Col. Ethan Allen, served until Dec. 1775.

Enlisted again in March 1776 under Capt. Jere Parmley, Col. Samuel Elmore and served one year.

Was in the battle of Ticonderoga; in garrison at Fort Schuyler and Fort Stanwix; a resident of Burton, Ohio, born 1756, died 1840.

FRANK, MRS. HELEN DUNNING, Nat. No.
  21,262, Painesville, O. Withdrawn.

Great-great-granddaughter of David Beach, who enlisted June 12, 1775 as a private in Capt. Bostwick's company, Col. Charles Webb's seventh Conn. regt. The regiment was ordered to Boston Camps and assigned to Gen. Sullivan's Brigade at Winter Hill.

David Beach served until Dec. 21, 1775. His regiment was adopted as a Continental Regiment.

From Jan. 1, 1777 until Dec. 4, 1778 he was sergeant in the 3d Regt., Conn. Line., and was engaged in the battle of Germantown, Oct. 4, 1777. and wintered at Valley Forge; participated in the batte of Monmouth June 28, 1778 and at the storming of Stony Point July 5, 1779. He was promoted to a Lieutenancy Jan. 4, 1778 and continued in service to the end of the war. Was an original member of the Order of the Cincinnati.

GOODWIN, MARY C., Nat. No. 39,725, Chardon, O.

Great-granddaughter of Childs Taylor, who participated in the engagements at Germantown and Princeton; was also stationed at Ticonderoga and Montreal, Canada.

GRANT, MRS. SADIE M., Nat. No. 24,289, Painesville, O.

Great-great-granddaughter of Reuben Buchman, who was a private in a Massachusetts Regiment, and a pensioner. Pension granted March 4, 1831.

GRISWOLD, MRS. MARIA LOUISE, Nat. No. 27,843, Painesville, O.

Great-great-granddaughter of Benj. Carpenter, who as private answered to the "Lexington Alarm" marching from Rehoboth, R. I. His name appears in service during 1775-1777-1778 and 1780. His wife Lucy Allen was a sister of Ethan Allen.

HOXETT, MRS. CAROLINE AMELIA BROOKS, Nat. No. 24,893, Gilroy, Cal.

Granddaughter of Stephen Brooks, who was a private on the Lexington Alarm, roll of Captain William Whitcomb's Co., Col. Jas. Prescott's Regt., which marched on the alarm of Apr. 19, 1775 from Stow, Massachusetts; was also in Capt. Amasa Cranston's Co., stationed at White Plains.

Great-granddaughter of Luke Brooks, who

with his son also answered to the Lexington Alarm of Apr. 19, 1775, and was afterwards in Capt. Benj. Munroe's 6th Company, 4th Mass. regiment.

Great-granddaughter of Daniel Rugg Jr., who was First Lieutenant in Capt. John White Jr's. Co., Col. Josiah Whitney's (2nd Worcester Co.) Regt.; again his name appears as Lieutenant of Capt. William Greenleaf's company, Col. Josiah Whitney's regt.; then as Captain in 1st Company of 2nd Worcester Co., commanded by Col. Josiah Whitney. Served three years and more.

Great-granddaughter of Isaac Goodspeed, who was a private in Capt. Ephriam Stockwell's company who marched to Bennington to reinforce Gen. Stark. Served also in Capt. Benj. Nye's Company, Maj. Jonas Wilder's Regiment.

Residence Barre, Mass.

Great-granddaughter of John Whitcomb, who participated in the battle of Bunker Hill. Having received official notice that he had been made Maj. General, he was next in rank to the commander-in-chief (Gen. Putnam). This was a provincial appointment, but the Continental Congress on June 5, 1776, made him Brig. Gen. and Washington announced his intention of assigning him at once to the command of the forces in Mass., relieving Gen. Ward, who had resigned, but Gen. Whitcomb asked "to be excused on account of age and a diffidence of not being able to answer the expectations of Congress." Prior to the war he had been a member of the General Court for 20 years. In the French and Indian War he held the offices of Lieut. Col. and Col. Fought at Ticonderoga and in Crown Point expedition.

JEROME, MRS. LUCY E. D., Nat. No. 21,263,
        Painesville, O.

Great-granddaughter of Asa Sprague, whose

name appears with the rank of Corporal on the Lexington Alarm Roll of Capt. Ebenezer Mason's Co., which marched on the alarm of Apr. 19, 1775 from Spencer, Mass. It also appears with rank of Sergeant on Muster and Pay Roll of Capt. David Prouty's Co., Maj. Asa Baldwin's division of Worcester County Regiment, which marched to reinforce the Northern Army by order of Council of Sept. 22, 1777.

KEECH, MRS. MARY W. S., Nat. No. 33,056, Perry, O.

Great-great-granddaughter of Richard Sinclair of Barnstead, who served as Captain in Col. Thomas Bartlett's Regiment raised to join the Continental Army at West Point in 1780. Afterwards served in the capacity of Maj. and Col. of Militia. In 1760 during the French and Indian War Richard Sinclair enlisted in Capt. Jeremiah Marston's Co. and served until the close of the war.

Great-great-granddaughter of Wm. Wyman Sr. Great-granddaughter of Wm. Wyman Jr. Great-great-granddaughter of Nathan Eaton. Great-great-granddaughter of Silas Antisdel. Great-great-granddaughter of James Parker.

For military service see Mrs. Barrows.

KING, MRS. JANE S., Nat. No. 21,264, Painesville, O.

Great-great-granddaughter of Solomon Cutler, who was Captain on the Muster and Pay Roll of the officers and men of Enoch Hale's Regiment which marched from the counties of Cheshire and Hillsborough, N. H. at the requisition of Maj. General Gates to reinforce the army at Ticonderoga.

KING, MRS. JOSEPHINE, Nat. No. 33,057,
Painesville, O.

Great-granddaughter of Titus Hayes, who
was a private in Capt. Woodbridge's Company,
7th Regiment, Connecticut Line. Enlisted May
26, 1777 for three years. Fought at Germantown
Oct. 4, 1777 and at Montreal and Valley Forge,
1778-1779, and on June 28 following was present
at the battle of Monmouth.
Encamped during the summer at White
Plains.

KNAPP, MRS. MILDRED ARMSTRONG,
Nat. No. 41,058, Painesville, O.

Great-great-granddaughter of David Alden
Jr., who served as private in Col. Henry Jackson's Regt. (Mass), aged 22. A pensioner.
Great-great-great-granddaughter of David Alden Sr., who was a private in Capt. Benj. Phil-
lip's Co., Col. Elisha Porter's Regt., (Hampshire
County, Mass.) Enlisted July 10, 1777, and served in the Northern Department.

LAWRENCE, MARTHA ELIZABETH, Nat.
No. 31,053, Painesville, O.

Great-granddaughter of Elisha Sawyer Jr.,
who was First Lieutenant in Massachusetts Bay
Militia, in Lieut. Col. Ephraim Sawyer's Regiment, which marched as a reinforcement for the
Northern Army on Oct. 2, 1777; also marched
on an alarm at Bennington in August 1777.

McABEE, MRS. MARY GREEN, Nat. No.
27,842, Painesville, O.

Great-granddaughter of Charles Reichȧrt,
who was a soldier in the War of the Revolution
for Pennsylvania; a pensioner.

McKINSTRY, HARRIETT ELVIRA, Nat. No.
—— Painesville, O.

Great-great-granddaughter of Capt. Salmon
White, who was born at Bolton, Conn., and died
at Whately, Mass., June 21, 1815.

He served in the War of the Revolution, ap-
pearing first on a list of officers of Mass. Militia,
March 22, 1776. Commissioned Apr. 5, 1776,
Capt. of 12th Co., 2nd Hampshire Co. Regt.;
again in Col. Woodbridge's Regt. four days in
Aug. 1777, marched by order of Gen. Horatio
Gates for service in Northern Department; also
in Col. Ezra May's Regt. from Sept. 20 to Oct.
14, 1777, marched to Saratoga; again in Col.
Israel Chapin's Regt., July 6, 1778.

Great-granddaughter of Daniel Williams,
born in 1761, died at Clymer, N. Y., Feb. 15,
1846. He served for Mass. as private in Capt.
Christopher Bannister's Co., Col. David Wells'
Regt. from May 8 to July 8, 1777. Company
marched to Ticonderoga; again in Capt. John
Kirklands' Co., Col. John Dickenson's Regt., for
eight days service in Aug. 1777, marched to
Bennington on an alarm; in Capt. Benjamin
Bonney's Co., Col. Ezra May's Regt. from Sept.
20, 1777 to Oct. 14, 1777. Company marched to
Stillwater.

MOODEY, MRS. LYDIA STEELE, Nat. No.
21,268, Painesville, O.

Great-granddaughter of Benjamin Palmer,
who enlisted at Grafton, Mass. in 1782, under
Capt. Francis in the Mass. Regt. commanded by
Col. Tupper. During his service he was transferred to several different companies and regiments and when discharged June 30, 1784, it
was from the Company of Capt. Jackson in the
Regiment of Col. Sprout, at Westfield, N. Y.

He was under charge June 30, 1784 at West Point. Was for many years a pensioner. Great-great-granddaughter of Peter Clark, a soldier of the Revolution from New Hampshire. See Mrs. Richardson.

MUNGER, MRS. EMILY A. GILL, Nat. No. 13,686, Geneva, O.

Great-granddaughter of John Gill, who enlisted March 6, 1777 as private in Capt. Elijah Blackman's Company, Col. Henry Sherburn's Regiment of Connecticut.

Great-granddaughter of Benjamin Ely, who was born Dec. 25, 1730, and died Dec. 25, 1802. A representative to the State Legislature during the Revolutionary War. Was chosen by the Legislature Jan. 31, 1776 as 1st Major of 3rd Hampshire County Regiment. Again under Col. Timothy Robinson, his name appears as Major, marching Aug 21, 1776 to Ticonderoga, by order of Gen. Schuyler.

NOBLE, MRS. LYDIA P., Nat. No. 30,140, Painesville, O.

Granddaughter of Edward Paine, who was born at Bolton, Conn. in 1746. He served as Ensign, Lieutenant and Captain in Connecticut Militia throughout the war. Later he was Brigadier General of Militia in New York state.

He came to Ohio in 1797, in 1799 to Painesville, bringing his family in 1800. Painesville bears his name.

See biography elsewhere.

NYE, MRS. ELEANOR MURRAY, Nat. No. 37,015, Painesville, O.

Great-great-granddaughter of William Stuart, who was a private in Capt. William Campbell's Company, Seventh Battalion, Cumberland County Militia, under Col. James Purdy, May 1, 1780.

PAIGE, MRS. CAROLINE WILCOX, Nat. No. 31,809, Painesville, O.

Great-granddaughter of Dea. Abel Wilcox, a soldier in Capt. Bezelial Bristol's Company, which answered to the alarm of East Haven, Conn., July 7, 1779. Was one of the "commen" men during the war.

Great-granddaughter of Capt. Martin Lord, who was born in Saybrook, Conn., June 5, 1742, died Dec. 15, 1821, and was buried at Killingsworth, Conn. He was a Capt. in the 7th Regiment of the Connecticut Militia. This regiment was called out in the New Haven Alarm July 5, 1779, to repel General Tryon.

PEARL, MRS. NANCY DOTY, Nat. No. 40,578, Fulton, O.

"Real daughter" of Peter Doty, who served during the War of the Revolution in the New Jersey Militia; a pensioner. Born in France in 1757 and died near Mt. Vernon, O. in 1848, at the age of 90 years, 10 months, and thirteen days.

Mrs. Pearl was born Feb. 8, 1808, passing away in the fall of 1902, being nearly ninety-five years old. We mourn the loss of this, our oldest "real daughter."

RICHARDSON, MRS. LAURA ALEXANDER, Nat. No. 21,259, New York City.

Great-great-great-granddaughter of Peter Clark, who joined the Continental Army in 1775, in Lyndeboro, N. H., and that same year was com-

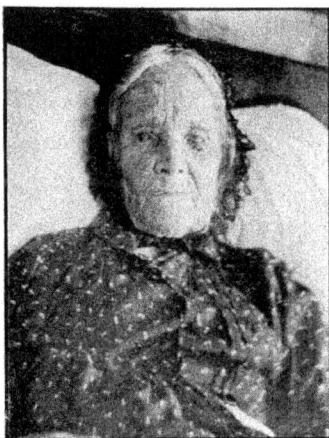

MRS. NANCY DOTY PEARL
(Nearly 95 Years Old)

MRS. SUSAN TRUBY

missioned Capt. of the 9th Regt., N. H. Millitia. He was engaged in the battle of Bennington, commanding sixty men. In this battle he showed great bravery, being second to scale the British breast works. He also took part in the defeat of Gen. Burgoyne at Saratoga in 1777.

Under the command of Lieut. Samuel Houston, he marched at the head of a company of men from Lyndeboro for Ticonderoga, July 1777. Was Capt. of a company in Col. Stickney's Regt., Gen. Stark's brigade of N. H. militia, which joined the Northern Continental Army. Capt. also of a company in Col. Daniel Moore's Regt. of volunteers which marched from Lyndeboro, Sept. 1777, and joined the Continental Army.

Great-great-granddaughter of Benjamin Palmer, a Revolutionary soldier from Massachusetts. See Mrs. Moodey.

SEARL, MRS. LIZZIE TISDEL, Nat. No. 21,266, Painesville, O.

Great-granddaughter of Silas Antisdel, who was a Private in Capt. Heath's Willington, Conn. Company; in Lexington Alarm.

Great-granddaughter of James Parker, who was a private in Capt. Dana's Company, Gen. Waterbury's Connecticut Brigade, under Gen. Washington at Phillipsburg.

Great-great-granddaughter of Col. Benj. Ely, who was a Major of the 3rd Hampshire Co., Mass. Regt., also Colonel of Militia; a Representative in the Legislature of Massachusetts.

SCOTT, MRS. EMMA ADAMS, Nat. No. 31,054, died at Painesville, O., Apr. 12, 1901.

Great-great-granddaughter of Moses Adams, who served three years in Massachusetts regi-

ments, with rank of Corporal and Sergeant.
Died June 28, 1778.

STOCKWELL, MRS. MARY AUGUSTA
AVERY, Nat. No. 20,035, Painesville, O.

Mrs. Stockwell organized the chapter and was
its first Regent.

Great-granddaughter of Jonathan Avery, who
served in the War of the Revolution as a private
in Capt. James Chapman's Co. of New London,
5th Co., 6th Regt.

This regiment was raised on the first call for
troops in Apr.-May 1775; was also a Sergeant,
and received a pension.

Great-granddaughter of John Pease, a Revolutionary soldier from Connecticut; a pensioner.
He served on Lake Champlain at Ticonderoga,
and in the retreat from Long Island into West
Chester Co., serving there under Gen. Washington.

TISDEL, MARY ELIZABETH, Nat. No.
21,267, Painesville, O.

Great-great-granddaughter of Silas Antisdel.
Great-great-granddaughter of James Parker.
Great-great-great-granddaughter of Col. Benj.
Ely.

For service of ancestry see Mrs. Searl.

TRUBY, MRS. SUSAN MURPHY, Nat. No.
27,844, Painesville, O.

"Real daughter" of Samuel Murphy, who enlisted in 1775 for one year in Eighth Virginia
Regiment; in 1777 for three years in Thirteenth
Virginia Regiment; in 1781 for one year in Virginia Militia; a pensioner.

Mrs. Truby was born in South Buffalo township, Armstrong County, Pennsylvania, June 28, 1810, is in fair health, and we hope will remain a "Real Daughter" for many years to come.

TUTTLE, NATALIE AGNES THOMPSON, Nat. No. 31,055, Painesville, O.

Great-granddaughter of Thomas Thompson, who served in the Continental Army in Capt. Cogswell's Co. (2nd), Col. Wessen's Regt. from Sept. 11, 1777 to Dec. 31, 1779.

Residence Halifax; also in Capt. W. Watson's Company, Col. Wessen's Regt. from Jan. 1, 1780 to June 1, 1780, enlisted again July 5, 1780, discharged Dec. 19, 1780.

His name appears on a list of men dated Camp Totoway Oct. 25, 1780, as passing muster.

Great-great-granddaughter of Joseph Call, who served in the Militia of Vermont in Capt. John Benjamin's Company, Col. Joseph Marsh's Regt. from Aug. 15 to Oct. 4, 1777.

He served on several scouting parties and alarms; he was appointed by the "Committee of Safety" to watch and guard suspected persons as enemies of the United States of America.

Great-great-great-granddaughter of Samuel Dutton Sr., of Littleton, Mass., who served in Capt. Samuel Reid's company of minute-men, Col. William Prescott's Regt., which marched on the alarm of Apr. 19, 1775.

Great-great-granddaughter of Samuel Dutton Jr., whose name appears in a list of men raised in Middlesex county for Continental service, residence Westford, engaged for the town of Westford, Mass.

Great-great-granddaughter of Richard Sinclair. For military service see Mrs. Keech.

TYLER, MRS. CAROLINE B., Nat. No. 13,688,
Geneva, O.

Great-granddaughter of Col. Benjamin Ely,
who was a Major of the 3rd Hampshire Co., Mass.
Regt., also Colonel of Militia; a representative in
the Legislature of Massachusetts.

Great-granddaughter of John Gill, who served
three years in Capt. Blackman's Company, Colonel Sherburne's Regiment, Connecticut Troops.

VIALL, MRS. ADA OSBORN, Nat. No. 21,269,
Painesville, O.

Great-great-granddaughter of Daniel Os-
borne, who, as private in Capt. Lemuel
Stoughton's company, marched from the town of
East Windsor, Conn., for the relief of Boston in
the Lexington Alarm, Apr. 1775. He was also
Sergeant in Capt. John Gray's company, Col.
Lemuel Whiting's Regt. Marched Oct. 5, 1777.

Great-great-granddaughter of Abner Prior,
who enlisted from Hartford, Conn., and whose
name appears as Captain in Maj. Bradley's Regt.;
and again as Major. He served in the French
and Indian War in 1755 and 1756.

Great-granddaughter of Stephen Brooks.
Great-great-granddaughter of Luke Brooks.
Great-great-granddaughter of Daniel Rugg Jr.
Great-great-granddaughter of Isaac Goodspeed.
Great-great-granddaughter of John Whitcomb.

For military service see Mrs. Hoxett.

WARREN, MRS. KATE T. M., Nat. No.
28,724, Painesville, O.

Great-great-granddaughter of Daniel Tilden,
who enlisted in the Conn. troops of the Revolutionary War at Lebanon, Conn., and served under Col. Durkee.

Daniel Tilden crossed the Delaware with

Washington. He was at Washington's side in crossing. After the battle of Lexington in 1775, a company went from Lebanon to aid in defence of Boston, and Daniel Tilden served as Captain nine days. In April or May 1775 he was 1st Lieut. with Capt. Little of 6th Co. of 3rd Regt., under Col. Israel Putnam until Dec. 10, 1775, and was at the battle of Bunker Hill. In 1776 the Regt. called Col. Durkee's was raised in which Daniel Tilden was Adjutant and promoted to Capt. Sept. 7, 1776.

On the first call for troops by the Legislature his Regiment marched from Boston to New York and was stationed at Bergen Heights and Paulus Hook, New Jersey until Sept. 15, 1776. He accompanied Washington in his retreat through New Jersey and was in the battle of Trenton, N. J., Dec. 25, 1776, and the battle of Princeton, Jan. 3, 1777.

Great-great-granddaughter of Joseph Loomis, who served as a Private from Connecticut in the War of the Revolution.

WILCOX, MARY E., Nat. No. 22,990, Painesville, O.

Great-granddaughter of Dea. Abel Wilcox, who served in an alarm at East Haven, Conn., July 7, 1779, in Captain Bezelial Bristol's Company.

Great-granddaughter of Capt. Martin Lord, who was born in Saybrook, Conn., Jan. 5, 1742.

WYMAN, MRS. MARY E. T., Nat. No. 21,270, Painesville, O.

Great-granddaughter of Silas Antisdel, who served in the Lexington Alarm.

Great-granddaughter of James Parker, who

served in Waterburg, Conn. Brigade under Washington at Phillipsburg.

Great-granddaughter of Col. Benjamin Ely, a Col. of Militia; a Representative in the Legislature of Mass. Residence West Springfield.

Great-granddaughter of John Gill, who served three years in Conn. Troops.

BIDWELL (cont.)
  Walter 10 Walter H 10
  William 9 William Sr 9 10
  Wm 10 Wm Jr 10
BIGELOW, 45
BISSELL, Benj 11 Benjamin
  11 11 Benjamin Sr 11
  Clark 11 Elizabeth 11 Mr
  11 Mrs 11
BLACKMAN, Capt 92 Elijah
  85
BLACKMON, Lucy
  Mathews 75
BLAIR, James 67
BLISH, Benj 53 Benjamin 11
  13 51 Phebe 11 Phoebe 51
BLISS, Anna 25 Capt 11
  Hannah 15
BLUCHER, Leonard 39
BONNEY, Benjamin 39 84
BOOTH, Henry 36
BOSTWICK, Capt 79
BRADLEY, Maj 92
  Thaddeus 63 79
BRADY, Samuel 27
BRANCH, Moses 79 William
  13-14
BRANT, Capt 57
BRASS, Garrit 14 Lucy 15
BREWER, David 8
BRIDGMAN, Elisha 63
BRIG, Capt 42
BRISTOL, Bezelial 86 93
BROOKS, David 32 Lovisa
  32 Luke 80 92 Stephen 80
  92

BROWN, Dauphin 15 Gracie
  15 Hannah 15-16 Hosea
  15 Lewis 15 Mrs 16
  Nabby 15 Oliver 15
  Patience 15 Zebulon 15
BUCHMAN, Reuben 80
BURGOYNE, 55 77 Gen 89
BURNHAM, Josiah 34
BURR, Aaron 46
BURROWS, Clara E
  Woodruff 76
BUSH, Richard 27
BUTLER, Col 46 Mrs 46
  Zebulon 11 14 43 77
CAHOON, William 16
CALFE, John 33
CALHOUN, J C 27
CALL, Joseph 16 91 Polly 21
  Rufus 17
CAMPBELL, Finley 25
  James 17 John 17 Mary 25
  William 86
CARD, Jonathan 17 Mr 17
  William 17
CARLL, John 67 Mary 67
CARLTON, Darius 63
CARPENTER, Annie Miller
  76 Benj 80 Ezra 17 Lucy
  80 Thomas 12
CARTER, Jabez 18 Jason 63
  Jonas 63
CHAPEL, Amos 7
CHAPIN, Israel 84
CHAPMAN, James 90
CHAPPELL, Lydia 67
  William 67

CHARLES II, King Of
England 21 51
CHEESEMAN, Isaac 63
CHESTER, John 19
CHURCH, Philemon 63
CILLEY, Col 7
CLAPP, Orris 12
CLARK, Ephraim 63 Isaac
63 Peter 85-86
CLAYE, Peter 18 78
CLEAVELAND, Moses 72
CLEVELAND, Phebe 19
Samuel 63 Tracy 18-19
CLIFT, Samuel 14
CLINTON, Gov 30
CLOCK, Col 36
COGSWELL, Capt 91
COLLACOTT, Mary Hove
76
COLSON, Christopher 18 78
COLTON, Charles 60 Isaac 8
COOK, Capt 36 Col 40
Marimon 66
CORNWALLIS, Lord 14
CRAINE, Abigail 19 Ahira
19 Alexis 19 Alvin 19
Cyrus 19 Eleazer 19
Horace 19 Roger 19-20
Ruth 19 Samuel 19 Sarah
19 Tower 19
CRANDALL, Amariah 20
Daniel 20 Elijah 20 Elisha
20 Prudence 20 Sarah 20
CRANSTON, Amasa 80
CRARY, Christopher 20-21
Oliver 20 Peter 21

CRARY (cont.)
Robert 21
CROMWELL, 51
CROSMAN, Robert 78
CROSSMAN, Robert 59
CULYER, Abraham 45
CUMINGS, Benj Sr 77 Julia
Alice 77 Stella Louise 77
CUNNINGHAM, Abigail 35
CURTIS, Maria Bethiah 8
CURTISS, Reuben 66
CUTLER, Solomon 82
DAGGETT, Col 18 John 26
31
DAMON, Abraham 66
DANA, Capt 89
DANIELS, 18
DANIELSON, Nellie V 78
DARROW, Adelia Field 78
DAVENPORT, Squire 66
DAY, Noah 34
DEAN, Thomas 75
DICKENSON, John 84
DIXON, Jonathan 44
DONALDSON, Samuel 66
DOTY, Peter 86
DOUGLAS, Col 44 Wm 59
DOWNS, Polly 58
DUNWELL, Stephen 67
DURAND, Andrew 66
DURKE, John 52
DURKEE, Col 92-93 John 13
DUTTON, Samuel Jr 91
Samuel Sr 91
EATON, Malinda 61 Nathan
61 75 82

EDDY, William R 21 Wm R
   21
EGESTON, Eiab 66
ELDRIDGE, Capt 15
ELLIOT, John 66
ELLIS, Lemuel 21 Polly 21
ELMORE, Samuel 79
ELY, Benj 89-90 Benjamin 85
   92 94
EMERSON, Joseph 22-23
   Lydia 23 Mary 23
EMERY, John 22
EMMS, Joshua 22
ENOS, Gen 61 Roger 33-34
   38
EVANS, Moses 23 Ora 23-24
FELLOWS, Parker 66
FERGUSON, John 24
   Leggett 25 Mary 25
FERRY, Spedy 59
FIELD, David 78 John 44
FISH, Capt 75 Jonathan 79
   Josiah 61
FLETCHER, Col 75 Samuel
   61
FOBES, Abigail 39 Asenath
   A 47 Lemuel 47 William
   47
FOOT, Aaron 58
FORBES, Anna 25 Lemuel 25
FORD, Andrew 25 Connie E
   79 Nathan 66
FOSTER, Lydia 23
FOWLER, Caleb 66 Mary M
   Donaldson 79
FOX, Israel 26 78

FRANCIS, Capt 84
FRANK, Helen Dunning 79
FRANKLIN, Joseph 26
FRENCH, Artemas 26
   Daniel I 26 Ezra 26 Mary
   26 Nathan 26 Seba 26
   Warren 26 William 26
FRYE, Col 23
FULLER, John 19 Joseph 27
   Joseph Sr 27 Rachel 27
GALLUP, Capt 73
GANSEVOORT, Peter 39
GANSON, Nathan 67
GARDNER, Jonathan 67
GATES, Horatio 84 Maj Gen
   82
GILL, John 85 92 94
GILSON, Daniel 66
GIRDLEY, Col 76
GOLDSMITH, 51 Jonathan
   34
GOODSPEED, Isaac 81 92
GOODWIN, Mary C 80
GORDON, Nathan 66
GRAHAM, Arter 67 Morris
   25
GRANT, Sadie M 80
GRAY, John 92
GREATON, John 40 60
GREEN, David 18 Ebenezer
   27 Ebenezer Jr 28 John 67
   Joseph 27-28
GREENLEAF, William 81
GRISWOLD, Maria Louise
   80
GROOME, Leah 39

HAGAR, Capt 57
HALE, Capt 26 78 Enoch 35
    82
HAMILTON, Gen 14
HAMLEN, Micah 11
HANKS, Benjamin 28
    Clorinda 28 Dea 29 Elijah
    28 Esther 28 John 28
    Joseph 28 Mary 28 Patty
    28
HARMON, Mary 29 Oliver
    29
HARPER, Alexander 22 29
    41 Col 30 John 30-31
HARRISON, Capt 51 Gen 46
HARVEY, Rhoda 45
HAYDEN, Samuel 30
HAYES, Seth 66 Titus 83
HEATH, Capt 8 89 Ebenezer
    75 Elizabeth 11
HEMINWAY, Samuel 67
HENDRIX, Warren B 38
HERKIMER, Gen 76 George
    76
HERRICK, Libens 66
HICKOX, Nathaniel 66
HICKS, Israel 12
HIGGIN, Solomon 22
HILL, Amasa 31 37 Jacob 77
HILTON, Mary 23
HINE, Augustus 54 Mary S
    54 Noble 73
HINMAN, Col 30
HOAG, Helen Bidwell 10
HODGES, Isaac 31 Samuel
    31 Simeon 31

HOLCOMB, D M 32 D R 32
    Fanny 32 Joel 32 Lovisa
    32 Marcus 32 Nancy 32
    Patience 15 Sally 32 Sarah
    32 Seymour 32
HOLLISTER, Asahel 32-33
    Mr 33
HOLMES, Margaret 62
HOMAN, Catherine 60
HOOKER, Col 58
HOOSE, George 38 Warren
    38
HOPKINS, Ebenezer 66
HORTON, Capt 45
HOSMER, Zachariah 66
HOUGHTON, Jonathan 8
HOUSTON, Samuel 89
HOUTON, Capt 35
HOW, Artemas 8
HOWE, Lord 55
HOXETT, Caroline Amelia
    Brooks 80 Mrs 92
HULL, Capt 9 William 56
HUNT, Thos 56
HUNTER, Samuel 28
HUNTINGTON, Jabez 76
    Jedediah 10
HUNTOON, Thomas 33
HUTCHIN, Capt 75
HUTCHINS, Moses 66
    William 61
HYDE, Jedediah 13
IDE, Jacob 18 Mary 26
JACKSON, Capt 84 Henry
    83
JEROME, Lucy E D 81

JEWETT, Joseph 9
JOHNSON, Benjamin 66
  Jonathan 66 Obadiah 41
JONES, Benaiah 33-34 51 53
  Benaiah Jr 33 Elkanah 34
  Jemima 33 51 Jemima
  Skinner 34 Mrs 34
JOY, Ebenezer 34-35
KEECH, Mary W S 82 Mrs
  91
KEEP, Capt 27
KENTFIELD, Ebenez 66
KIDDER, Reuben 66
KIMBALL, Abel 35 Abigail
  35 Lemuel 35 Mary 35
KING, Benjamin 66 Jane S 82
  Josephine 83
KINGSBURY, Joseph 77
  Lemuel 78
KIRKLANDS, John 84
KNAPP, Mildred Armstrong
  83
KNOX, Gen 74
KOCH, Elizabeth 36
LAFAYETTE, 20
LANE, Joseph 67
LATTIMORE, Robert 34
LAWRENCE, Col 7 Martha
  Elizabeth 83
LEDYARD, Col 11 Wm 34
LEE, Capt 56 Thomas 29
LEFFINGWELL, Capt 13
LEONARD, Capt 54
LESTER, Benajah 73 Samuel
  Jr 73
LITTLE, Capt 93

LOCK, Joseph 54
LOOMIS, Amasa 51 73
  Joseph 93
LORD, Martin 86 93
LOVELAND, Frederick 66
LYMAN, Col 23
LYON, Zebuon 16
MALADY, Aaron 17
MALCOLM, William 42
MARCY, Capt 75
MARION, Jonathan 8
MARKELL, Benjamin 36
  Betsey 36 Elizabeth 36
  Fanny 36 Henry 37 James
  36 John 36 Margarette 36
  Mary 36 Nancy 36
  Nicholas 36 Peter 36-37
MARSH, Joseph 16 91
MARSHALL, Seth 57
  Thomas 11
MARSTON, Jeremiah 82
MARTIN, Isaac 37 Sylvanus
  11
MASON, 46 Ebenezer 82
MASTICK, Benjamin 66
MATTHEWS, Lucy 15
MATTICE, Hannah 57
MAY, Ezra 84
MCABEE, Mary Green 83
MCCLELLAN, Col 35
MCINTOSH, William 21
MCKINSTRY, Harriet Elvira
  84
MEAD, John 31
MERINER, Ephraim 7
MERRY, Esq 13

MESSENGER, Anna 38
  Ashbel 38 Isaac 37-38
  Reuben 38
MILLER, Rachel 27
MILLS, I A Branch 14 Ida A
  9
MIX, Capt 58
MIXER, Abigail 39 Phineas
  38 Phineas Jr 39 Phineas
  Sr 38
MOODEY, Lydia Steele 84
  Mrs 89
MOONEY, Col 35
MOORE, Daniel 89 Isaac 39
  John 39 John 3d 39 Leah
  39 Mrs 39
MORGAN, Col 57 Daniel 66
  Ezra 36 Nancy 36
MORLEY, Ezekiel 40-41 Mr
  40 Mrs 40 Thomas 40
MORSE, Benj 41 Benjamin
  41
MOTT, Edward 74
MUNGER, Emily A Gill 85
MUNROE, Benj 81
MUNSON, Capt 11
MURPHY, Samuel 74 90
NEWEL, Col 15
NICHOLS, Capt 35 Col 35
  Jonas 42 Phineas 42
NIXON, Thomas 77
NOBLE, Lydia P 85
NORTHRUP, Stephen 66
NORWOOD, Stephen 42
NYE, Benj 81 Eleanor
  Murray 85

OSBORN, Capt 55
OSBORNE, Daniel 92
OSGOOD, Aaron 23
PAIGE, Caroline Wilcox 86
PAINE, Aurel Ellsworth 43
  Col 52 Edward 42 52 72
  77 85 Eleazer 43 77 Gen
  47 57 Mr 43 Rebecca
  White 42 Stephen 43 77
PAIR, Capt 57
PALMER, Benjamin 84 89 D
  L 32 Elijah 20
PARKER, James 75 82 89-90
  93 Mary 35
PARKS, Amaziah 43 Nathan
  66 Sabra 44
PARMLEY, James L 56 Jere
  79
PARRISH, Cyprian 67
PARSON, Samuel Holding
  74
PATCH, Elisha 32 Sally 32
PAYNE, H B 53
PEARL, Mrs 86 Nancy Doty
  86
PEASE, Isaac 66 John 90
PENOYER, Jonathan 7
PEPOON, Joseph 53
PERKINS, Hannah 16
PERRY, Nathan 53 Paulina
  53-54
PHELPS, Capt 26 78
  Elizabeth Stuart 51 Ira 66
  Seth 66
PHILLIPS, Benj 83
PIERCE, Daniel 17

PIKE, Capt 67 Sally 45
PITCHER, Benj 44 Mr 44
PLUMB, Mary 29
POMEROY, Daniel 66
    Ichabod 66
POOL, Jepthah 66
POOLE, William 78
POOR, Enoch 33
POPE, Eliza Dorcas 39
PORTER, Elisha 83 Noah 10
POTTER, Borden 66
PRATT, Jonathan 67
PRESCOTT, Jas 80 William
    23 91
PRIOR, Abner 92
PROUTY, David 82
PURDY, James 86
PUTNAM, Gen 81 Israel 41
    93
QUIGGLE, Peter 66
REICHERT, Charles 83
REID, Samuel 91
REYNOLDS, John 44
RICHARDS, Lieut Col 20
    Samuel 45
RICHARDSON, Laura
    Alexander 86 Mrs 85
RIDER, Benjamin 66
RIGDON, Sidney 35
ROBINSON, Thos 28
    Timothy 85
ROBISON, Oliver 67
ROGERS, Col 45 Rhoda 45
    Sally 45 Samuel 45
ROSA, Agnes 45 Isaac 45
    Storm 45

ROSS, 12
RUGG, Daniel Jr 81 92
RUSSELL, Gideon 66
SABIN, Col 58
SAFFORD, Jesse 16
SAINTCLAIR, 46 Gov 43
SARGENT, Paul Dudley 21
SAWYER, Elisha Jr 83
    Ephraim 83 James 23
SCHUYLER, Gen 85
SCOTT, Emma Adams 89
SEARL, Lizzie Tisdel 89 Mrs
    90
SEARLS, Nabby 15
SEDGEWICK, Capt 30
SESSIONS, Anson 45-47
    Asenath A 47 Aurel 47
    Horace 48 Mariner 47 Mr
    46-47 Mrs 47 Norman 47
    Sgt 46
SHEFFIELD, Capt 20
SHELDON, Capt 54
SHEPARD, William 27
SHEPHERD, Col 19
SHERBURN, Henry 85
SHERBURNE, Col 92
SHERWOOD, Malvina 30
SIMMONS, Peleg 48
SINCLAIR, Richard 82 91
SKINNER, Abraham 11 43
    51 73 Abram 51 Capt 12
    52-54 Jemima 33 51 John
    34 Mary 52 Mary S 54
    Paulina 53-54 Phebe 11
    Phoebe 51
SLOAN, Samuel 16

102

WARD, Anna 38 Gen 81
WARNER, Joseph 25 Sarah
32
WARREN, Kate T M 92
WASHBURN, Abel 32
Nancy 32
WASHINGTON, 19-20 33 38
71 75 81 93-94 Gen 13-15
24 55 74 89-90 Mrs 55
WATERBURY, Brig Gen 75
Gen 89
WATSON, W 91
WAYNE, Gen 46
WEBB, Charles 79
WELCH, Gracie 15
WELD, Col 21
WELLS, Capt 40 David 84
Timothy 67
WESSEN, Col 91
WHEELER, Abi 58
WHITAKER, John 77
WHITCOMB, Gen 81 John
81 92 William 80
WHITE, John Jr 81 Salmon
84
WHITING, Frederick Jones
74 Lemuel 92
WHITNEY, Capt 75 Josiah 8
81
WHITON, Sarah 19

WHITTLESEY, Elisha 30
WILCOX, Abel 86 93
Elnathan 67 Mary E 93
WILDER, Jonas 81
WILLIAMS, Capt 29 Col 12
Daniel 84 George 59 78
Joseph 40
WILSON, Ebenezer 59 78
Israel 67 Samuel 59
WIRT, Catherine 60 Jacob 60
Martin 59 Samuel 50
WITTER, Joseph 67
WOLFF, Jacob 74
WOOD, John 21
WOODBRIDGE, Capt 83
Col 26 54 78 84
WOODRUFF, Gedor 76
WOODWORTH, Ezekiel 60-
61 Harvey 61 James 61
WOOSTER, Gen 37
WRIGHT, Elijah 32 34 Fanny
32 James 32 Job 24 Josiah
79 Thomas L 9
WYLLY, Samuel 28 32
WYMAN, Don 8 62 Guy 62
Henry 62 Malinda 61
Margaret 62 Mary E T 93
William 61-62 William Jr
62 75 William Sr 62 75
Wm Jr 61 75 82 Wm Sr 82

www.ingramcontent.com/pod-product-compliance
Lightning Source LLC
Chambersburg PA
CBHW071059090426
42737CB00013B/2395